Guide to SEC Privacy Rules

Broker-Dealers, Investment Companies and Advisers

Related CCH Titles

Financial Privacy Law Guide

Investment Adviser Newsletter

Mutual Funds Guide

Managing Marketeers: Supervisory Responsibilities of Broker-Dealers and Investment Advisers

Guide to SEC Privacy Rules

Broker-Dealers, Investment Companies and Advisers

James Hamilton, J.D., LL.M.
Ted Trautmann, J.D.

CCH INCORPORATED
Chicago

EDITORIAL STAFF

James Hamilton, J.D., LL.M.

Ted Trautmann, J.D.

ISBN: 0-8080-0733-5

4025 West Peterson Avenue
Chicago, IL 60645-6085
1-800-248-3248
http://business.cch.com

FOREWORD

The Gramm-Leach-Bliley Act represents the most sweeping reform of financial services regulation in over 60 years. One of its many important accomplishments was to establish a minimum federal standard of financial privacy. Under the Act, brokers, dealers, investment companies, and registered investment advisers, regardless of their size, must have written privacy policies and must disclose them to customers. This disclosure must take place when a customer relationship is established and not less than annually during the continuation of the relationship.

As the federal functional regulator of brokers, dealers, investment companies, and investment advisers, the Securities and Exchange Commission has adopted privacy rules for this regulated community. Fulfilling its Gramm-Leach-Bliley mandate, the SEC adopted Regulation S-P, which took effect in November 2000. Compliance with the rules was made mandatory by July 1, 2001.

This guide discusses the SEC's privacy rules, placing them in the context of the Gramm-Leach-Bliley Act's privacy provisions. The guide explains the initial, annual, and opt-out notices required by the Act and the rules, and the specific information that these notices must contain. It also discusses the means of delivering notices, limits on disclosure of personal information to third parties, and various exceptions to the opt-out requirements for such activities as joint marketing and processing and servicing transactions. In addition, the guide includes extensive discussion of the definitional provisions in the rules, as well as practical guidance issued by the SEC for certain financial institutions. Finally, the guide reproduces the full text of the rules themselves, along with an appendix of sample privacy clauses that accompanies those rules.

November 2001

Table of Contents

Explanation—SEC Privacy Rules

Introduction and Scope . . . . . ¶ 101
Examples, Sample Clauses and Safe Harbors . . . . . ¶ 102
Definitions . . . . . ¶ 103
Initial Privacy Notice . . . . . ¶ 104
Annual Privacy Notice . . . . . ¶ 105
Contents of Annual and Initial Notices . . . . . ¶ 106
Opt-Out Notice . . . . . ¶ 107
Revised Privacy Notice . . . . . ¶ 108
Means of Delivering Notices . . . . . ¶ 109
Limits on Disclosure to Third Parties . . . . . ¶ 110
Opt-Out Exceptions for Joint Marketing . . . . . ¶ 111
Exceptions for Processing and Servicing Transactions . . . . . ¶ 112
Other Exceptions to Opt-Out Requirements . . . . . ¶ 113
Limits on Redisclosure and Reuse . . . . . ¶ 114
Limits on Sharing Account Number Information . . . . . ¶ 115
Fair Credit Reporting Act . . . . . ¶ 116
State Laws . . . . . ¶ 117
Privacy Protection Standards . . . . . ¶ 118
Guidance for Certain Entities . . . . . ¶ 119

Appendix—Regulation S-P

17 CFR § 248.1 . . . . . ¶ 201
17 CFR § 248.2 . . . . . ¶ 202
17 CFR § 248.3 . . . . . ¶ 203
17 CFR § 248.4 . . . . . ¶ 204
17 CFR § 248.5 . . . . . ¶ 205
17 CFR § 248.6 . . . . . ¶ 206
17 CFR § 248.7 . . . . . ¶ 207
17 CFR § 248.8 . . . . . ¶ 208
17 CFR § 248.9 . . . . . ¶ 209
17 CFR § 248.10 . . . . . ¶ 210
17 CFR § 248.11 . . . . . ¶ 211

17 CFR § 248.12 . . . . ¶ 212
17 CFR § 248.13 . . . . ¶ 213
17 CFR § 248.14 . . . . ¶ 214
17 CFR § 248.15 . . . . ¶ 215
17 CFR § 248.16 . . . . ¶ 216
17 CFR § 248.17 . . . . ¶ 217
17 CFR § 248.18 . . . . ¶ 218
17 CFR § 248.30 . . . . ¶ 219
Appendix—Sample Clauses . . . . ¶ 220

Topical Index . . . . page 89

SEC Privacy Rules

¶ 101 Introduction and Scope

At the direction of Congress, the SEC has adopted rules to implement the mandates of the Gramm-Leach-Bliley Act's privacy provisions. The rules, which cover the privacy policies of broker-dealers, investment companies, and registered investment advisers, were adopted in conjunction with other federal financial regulators, including the banking regulators and the Federal Trade Commission.

The recently enacted Gramm-Leach-Bliley Act allows the creation of new financial services holding companies that can offer a full range of banking, securities and insurance products under a strong regulatory regime based on the principle of functional regulation. The Act also established a minimum federal standard of privacy to protect a consumer's personal financial information. Regulators, including the SEC, were directed to establish comprehensive privacy standards.

As mandated by Gramm-Leach-Bliley, the SEC has adopted rules (Regulation S-P, 17 CFR § 248.1 et seq.) to require brokers, dealers, investment companies, and investment advisers to disclose their privacy policies to customers initially and annually during the customer relationship. The rules also require the financial institutions to protect customer information and provide opt-out notices if the institutions plan to share consumer information with non-affiliated third parties. The SEC estimates that approximately 5500 broker-dealers, 4300 investment companies, and 8100 investment advisers are subject to the privacy rules.

As more fully explained below, the SEC rules have three main purposes. First, they require a financial institution to provide notice to consumers about its privacy policies and practices (see ¶ ¶ 104 and 105). Second, the rules describe the conditions under which a financial institution may disclose nonpublic personal information about a consumer to a non-affiliated third party (see ¶ 110). Third, the rules provide a method for consumers to opt out of the disclosure of that information to third parties, subject to a number of exceptions (see ¶ 107).

Brokers and Dealers

The SEC privacy rules sweep into their embrace a large collection of financial institutions that the Commission functionally regulates. For example, the rules define "broker" as having the same meaning as in Exchange Act Section 3(a)(4), whether or not the institution is registered under Section 15(b) of the Act. The term also includes municipal securities brokers and government securities brokers. Similarly, the rules define "dealer" as having the same meaning as Exchange Act Section 3(a)(5), whether or not the dealer is registered under the Act. The term also includes municipal securities dealers and government securities dealers.

Investment Companies

Regarding investment companies, the privacy rules incorporate the meaning of investment company in Section 3 of the Investment Company Act, whether or not the company is registered with the SEC. Thus, a business development company, which is an investment company but is not required to register with the SEC, would be subject to the privacy provisions. The definition also clarifies that the term includes a separate series of an investment company.

But note that the SEC privacy rules do not apply to hedge funds satisfying the criteria for exclusion from regulation under Sections 3(c)(1) or 3(c)(7) of the Investment Company Act.

Investment Advisers

The definition of "investment adviser" incorporates the definition found in Investment Advisers Act Section 202(a)(11). Only registered investment advisers are covered by the SEC's privacy rules.

Insurance Products

The Gramm-Leach-Bliley Act excludes insurance companies from the SEC's enforcement and rulemaking authority. The SEC believes that the Act relies on the states to enforce its privacy provisions with regard to any insurance activities conducted by broker-dealers, funds, and investment advisers.

Consistent with this statutory reading, the SEC excluded the provision of insurance by a broker-dealer, mutual fund, or adviser from the scope of Regulation S-P. If the insurance product is also a security, however, any brokerage firm or mutual fund providing that security, or investment adviser providing advice regarding that security, is subject to the SEC privacy rules. In addition, insurance company separate accounts that are investment companies are subject to the privacy rules.

Variable annuities and variable life insurance contracts are examples of insurance products that are also securities. With regard to these products, the customer for privacy rule purposes is the policyholder not the beneficiary. For example, the purchaser of a variable annuity forms a customer relationship with the financial institution that sold the annuity. The person obtaining the product or service from the financial institution is the person purchasing the annuity. These individuals could include a contract owner and could also include any other individual who has the rights of a contract owner, such as the ability to direct underlying investments.

Foreign Institutions

The privacy rules apply to any broker-dealer, mutual fund, or registered investment adviser regardless of whether its consumers are U.S. persons or non-U.S. persons and regardless of whether its activities are conducted through foreign or domestic offices or branches. Thus, the privacy rules apply to the foreign offices of registered broker-dealers, funds, and advisers, in addition to their domestic offices.

The rules do not, however, apply to foreign broker-dealers or funds that are not registered with the SEC. Despite the broad reach of the federal securities laws, the SEC believes it impractical to apply the rules to these entities. If a foreign broker or mutual fund conducts activities through U.S. commerce in a manner subjecting it to the registration provisions of the federal securities laws, it is subject to those provisions as well as to the antifraud provisions.

The SEC concluded that placing a duty on these unregistered firms to provide privacy and opt-out notices would not add to investor protection under Gramm-Leach-Bliley. But if a foreign broker or fund or adviser decides to register with the Commission, it would have to comply fully with the privacy rules.

The SEC has noted that other federal, state, or even applicable foreign law may impose limitations on disclosures of nonpublic personal information in addition to those imposed by the Gramm-Leach-Bliley Act and the SEC's rules. For example, an investment adviser may be subject to fiduciary principles under state law that impose additional limits on the adviser's ability to disclose information about its customers to any third party. Thus, the Commission advises financial institutions to monitor and comply with relevant legislative and statutory developments affecting the disclosure of consumer information.

¶ 102 Examples, Sample Clauses and Safe Harbors

Given the wide variety of transactions covered by the Gramm-Leach-Bliley privacy provisions, the SEC rules include examples intended to assist financial institutions in complying with the rules (see, *e.g.*, Rule 248.3(c)(2), at ¶ 203). These examples are not intended to be exhaustive, but are rather intended to provide guidance about how the rules are likely to apply in specific situations.

The SEC has also included sample clauses to assist firms in drafting privacy notices (see Regulation S-P Appendix, reproduced at ¶ 220). The sample clauses are provided to illustrate the appropriate level of detail. Financial institutions are cautioned against relying on the sample disclosures without determining the relevance or appropriateness of the disclosure to their operations. Statutory terms such as "nonpublic personal information" and "non-affiliated third parties" in the sample clauses are used to generally convey the subject of the clauses.

A firm using these terms, however, must provide sufficient information to enable consumers to understand what those terms mean in the context of the institution's notices. The sample disclosures address solely the level of detail required and do not try to provide guidance on issues such as type size, margin width, or other characteristics affecting whether a notice is clear and conspicuous.

Although commenters had urged the SEC to follow the approach taken by the banking regulators and give the examples the force and legal effect of a safe harbor, the Commission reiterated that the examples and the sample clauses do not provide a safe harbor. Rather, the examples describe ordinary situations that would comply with the applicable rule. But the particular facts and circumstances relating to each specific situation will determine if compliance with an example or use of a sample clause is tantamount to compliance with the rule.

Nevertheless, the SEC believes that, when read together, the examples and sample clauses provide broker-dealers, funds, and investment advisers with sufficient guidance on ways to comply with the rules as well as sufficient flexibility to comply with the regulation in ways appropriate for the institution.

¶ 103 Definitions

The Gramm-Leach-Bliley Act privacy provisions and the SEC privacy rules contain a number of important terms of art. The SEC has extensively defined a number of these terms, and it is helpful to examine these definitions before examining the substantive mandates of the rules.

Clear and Conspicuous

Both Gramm-Leach-Bliley and the SEC rules require that various privacy notices that financial institutions must give consumers be "clear and conspicuous." The SEC defines this term to mean that the notice is reasonably understandable and designed to call attention to the nature and significance of the information contained in the notice (see Rule 248.3(c), at ¶ 203). This standard is designed to generate notices to consumers that effectively communicate the information they need to make an informed choice about the privacy of their information, including whether to open a brokerage account, buy shares in a mutual fund, or engage an investment adviser.

The rules do not mandate the use of any particular technique for making the notices clear and conspicuous, but rather allow each financial institution the flexibility to decide for itself how best to comply with this requirement. A notice could satisfy the clear and conspicuous standard, for example, by using a plain language caption, in a type-set easily read, that is designed to call attention to the information contained in the notice. Other plain language principles are provided in the examples following the general rule.

The SEC examples are designed to guide firms through the "reasonably understandable" and "call attention to" components of the clear and conspicuous standard. A firm makes its privacy notice reasonably understandable if it:

- Presents information in clear and concise sentences, paragraphs, and sections;
- Uses short explanatory sentences or bullet lists whenever possible;
- Uses definite and concrete everyday words and active voice whenever possible;
- Avoids multiple negatives;
- Avoids legal and highly technical business terminology whenever possible, and;
- Avoids imprecise explanations readily subject to different interpretations (Rule 248.3(c)(2)(i), at ¶ 203).

A privacy notice is designed to call attention to the nature and significance of the enclosed information if it:

- Uses a plain language heading;
- Uses easy-to-read typefaces and type sizes;
- Provides wide margins and ample line spacing;
- Uses boldface or italics for key words; and
- Uses distinctive type size, style, and graphics, such as shading or sidebars when combined with other information (Rule 248.3(c)(2)(ii), at ¶ 203).

The SEC acknowledges that many of the above examples are imprecise. The agency believed that more prescriptive examples would be inappropriate in a given circumstance. To avoid this result, the examples provide generally applicable guidance about ways in which a broker or a fund or an adviser may make a disclosure clear and conspicuous. At the end of the day, a firm must decide for itself how best to comply and may, in doing so, use techniques not listed in the examples

Combining privacy notice with another document

The privacy rules do not prohibit a financial institution from combining a privacy notice with another document. Thus, an initial or annual privacy notice can be incorporated into another document, such as an account statement, annual report, prospectus, trade confirmation, Form ADV, or adviser's brochure. Any privacy notice, however, must be clear and conspicuous. Therefore, the SEC requires that a privacy notice combined with another document be distinct from and not hidden in other information in the document. In addition, a financial institution must deliver a privacy notice to customers each year even if other information in the combined document need not be delivered annually, such as an investment adviser's brochure.

Since privacy disclosure may be clear and conspicuous even when it is combined with other disclosures, the rules do not require that it be on a separate piece of paper. Thus, a document may combine a privacy notice with other disclosures subject to a different regulatory regime. For example, a mutual fund could include a clear and conspicuous privacy notice in a prospectus prepared under Securities Act standards. The SEC rules provide that, when a privacy notice is combined with other information, the notice must use a distinctive type size, style, and graphics, such as shading and sidebars.

To avoid the potential conflicts between two different rules requiring different sets of disclosures subject to different standards, the SEC rules do not mandate precise specifications for presenting various disclosures.

Internet

Presenting clear and conspicuous privacy disclosures on the Internet presents unique issues. Consumers may view various web pages within a firm's web site in a different order each time they access the site, aided by hyperlinks. Depending on the hardware and software used to access the Internet, some web pages may require consumers to scroll down to view the entire page.

The SEC examples address these issues by providing that a firm may comply if it uses text or visual cues to encourage scrolling down the page if necessary to view the entire notice and ensure that other elements on the web site, such as text, graphics, hyperlinks, and sound, do not distract attention from the notice. The examples also urge firms to place a notice or a conspicuous link on a screen that consumers frequently access, such as on a page on which consumers conduct transactions.

A firm could use a range of approaches in complying. For example, a broker-dealer could use a dialog box that pops up to provide the disclosure before a consumer provides information to a financial institution. Another approach would be a simple, clearly labeled graphic located near the top of the page or in close proximity to the firm's logo, directing the customer through a hyperlink to the privacy disclosures on a separate web page.

Consumers

There is a significant distinction between the duties a broker, dealer, mutual fund or adviser owes a consumer and the duties owed to a customer.

Both the Gramm-Leach-Bliley Act and the SEC privacy rules distinguish consumers from customers for purposes of the Act's notice requirements.

A financial institution must give a consumer the notices required under the Act's privacy provisions only if it intends to disclose nonpublic personal information about the consumer to a non-affiliated third party for a purpose not authorized by one of the exceptions. By contrast, a financial institution must give privacy notices to all customers at the time of establishing a customer relationship and annually thereafter during the relationship's continuation.

It can be seen that the consumer relationship will place no additional burden on a financial institution if no customer relationship is established and the institution does not intend to disclose nonpublic personal information about the consumer to third parties.

Thus, a financial institution is under no obligation to provide a consumer who is not a customer with any privacy disclosures unless it intends to disclose the consumer's personal information to a third party. And the institution can disclose such information to third parties if it delivers the requisite notices and the consumer does not opt out.

The rules allow a financial institution to avoid all requirements for consumers who are not customers if the institution chooses not to share information about consumers with non-affiliated third parties. Conversely, if a financial institution chooses to share a consumer's nonpublic personal information with third parties, the institution is free to do so provided it tells consumers about the sharing and gives them a reasonable opportunity to opt out. In this way, the SEC is attempting to strike a balance between protecting an individual's personal information and minimizing the burden on financial institutions.

The SEC defines a "consumer" as an individual who obtains from a financial institution products and services for primarily personal, family, or household purposes (Rule 248.3(g)(1), at ¶ 203). The definition also includes an individual's legal representative. Under this seemingly straightforward definition lurk difficult questions involving the "consumer" status of applicants for financial services and trust beneficiaries. There is also the question of whether individuals can be consumers of institutions holding ownership or servicing rights to their loans.

Applicant for financial services

A consumer is also an individual who provides nonpublic personal information when applying for brokerage or investment advisory services, even if the application is denied or withdrawn. This is so because a financial product or service includes a broker or adviser's evaluation of an application to obtain a financial product or service.

For example, an investor who provides nonpublic personal information to several registered advisers (whether orally or in writing) in seeking financial advisory services would be a consumer of each registered adviser, even if the investor does not enter into an advisory contract with any of the advisers.

Brokers, mutual funds, and investment advisers frequently provide a range of services in connection with the delivery of a financial product, including the evaluation of information provided by an individual. The evaluation may be the sole financial product or service delivered, or one of several services provided in connection with establishing a customer relationship.

For example, an investor who seeks to invest in stock options must provide nonpublic personal information in connection with the request. Based on this information, the broker or adviser may open an account for the investor, but deny his or her request to invest in options. Whether the evaluation is the sole product or service or one of several, the evaluation of the individual's information is a separate financial product or service.

This result, in the SEC's view, is consistent with one of the primary purposes of Gramm-Leach-Bliley's privacy provisions, which is to enable individuals to restrict a financial institution from sharing nonpublic personal information about them with a nonaffiliated third party.

The information provided to a financial institution before the establishment of a customer relationship will likely contain precisely the types of information that the statute seeks to protect. This information is no less deserving of protection simply because an application is denied or withdrawn.

Loans

The SEC rules provide that a person will be a consumer of any entity that holds ownership or servicing rights to an individual's loan. But note that those consumers may not be customers (see discussion below explaining how the definition of "customer" will be applied in the loan context).

Regarding consumers, the Commission believes that financial institutions that own or service a loan provide a financial product or service to the individual borrower in question. In some cases, the product or service is the funding of the loan, directly or indirectly. In other cases, the product or service is the processing of payments, sending account-related notices, responding to consumer questions about the handling of the account. The definition of a consumer covers individuals receiving products or services in each of these situations.

An individual will not be considered a consumer of an entity acting as agent for a financial institution. The broker, fund, or adviser has a consumer relationship with the individual even if it uses agents to help it deliver its products and services. For example, fund consumers would not become consumers of the transfer agent that services the fund's accounts.

Similarly, an individual who has an account with an introducing broker and whose securities are carried by a clearing broker in a special omnibus account in the name of the introducing broker is not a consumer for purposes of the clearing broker who receives only the account numbers and transaction information in order to clear transactions.

Also, investment company shareholders who are not the record owners of their shares would not be consumers for purposes of the investment company.

Trusts

Gramm-Leach-Bliley's definition of "consumer" does not squarely resolve whether the beneficiary of a trust is a consumer of the financial institution that serves as trustee. The SEC believes that, when the financial institution serves as trustee of a trust, neither the grantor nor beneficiary is a consumer or customer under the rules. Instead, the trust itself is the entity that obtains the financial services, and the rules do not apply because the trust is not an individual. Similarly, a trust, partnership, or personal corporation that has an account with a broker-dealer, fund, or adviser would not be a customer for purposes of the privacy rules because these entities are not individuals.

A financial institution serving as a trustee assumes obligations as a fiduciary, including the duty to protect the confidentiality of the beneficiaries' information, that are consistent with the purposes of Gramm-Leach-Bliley and enforceable under state law. Thus, the SEC has excluded an individual who is a beneficiary of a trust or a plan participant in an employee benefit plan from the definitions of "consumer" and "customer." The SEC believes, however, that an individual who selects a financial institution to be a custodian of securities or assets in an individual retirement account is a GLB consumer.

Examples

The following are examples of individuals who are *not* consumers:

- An individual who provides a firm with only name, address, and general areas of investment interest in connection with a request for a prospectus, an investment adviser brochure, or other information about financial products or services.

- An individual who has an account with another broker or dealer (the introducing broker-dealer) that carries securities for the individual in a special omnibus account with the clearing broker-dealer in the name of the introducing broker-dealer, and when the clearing firm receives only the account numbers and transaction information of the introducing broker-dealer's consumers in order to clear transactions.

- A purchaser of mutual fund shares issued only through a broker or dealer or investment adviser who is the record owner of those shares is not a consumer of the fund.

- A consumer of financial institution does not become a consumer of a firm that acts as agent for, or provide processing or other services to, that financial institution (Rule 248.3(g)(2), at ¶ 203).

Use of Internet financial tools

At times, people will use a financial tool that a financial institution makes available on the Internet. Generally, these tools are used on a one-time or sporadic basis and users are not required to enter their names and addresses. Thus, the information provided through the Internet tool is not personally identifiable. Under these circumstances, the individual using the tool would not be the institution's consumer.

Consumer Reporting Agency

Regulation S-P incorporates the definition of "consumer reporting agency" in Section 603(f) of the Fair Credit Reporting Act (Rule 248.3(h), at ¶ 203).

Customers

The term "customer" means any consumer who has a customer relationship with a financial institution (Rule 248.3(j), at ¶ 203). Thus, consumers become customers when they enter into a continuing relationship with the institution. For example, consumers become customers when they enter into a written or oral investment advisory contract, complete documents necessary to open a brokerage account, or buy shares of an investment company in their own names.

The distinction between consumers and customers determines the notices that a financial institution must provide. If a consumer never becomes a customer, the institution does not have to provide any notices to the consumer unless it intends to disclose the consumer's nonpublic personal information to a non-affiliated third party.

By contrast, if a consumer becomes a customer, the SEC rules require that the institution provide a copy of its privacy policy when it establishes the customer relationship and at least annually during the continuation of that relationship.

The SEC defines "customer relationship" to be a continuing relationship between a consumer and a financial institution in which the institution provides a financial product or service that is to be used by the consumer primarily for personal, family, or household purposes (Rule 248.3(k)(1), at ¶ 203). Consumers have a continuing relationship with a financial institution if they have a brokerage account or an investment advisory account with the institution, or if they are record owners of shares issued by an investment company.

There is a customer relationship if the institution holds securities or other assets as collateral for a loan made to the consumer, even if the institution neither made the loan nor effected any transaction on the consumer's behalf. Similarly, a financial institution has a customer relationship with consumers that have accounts with introducing brokers that clear transactions with and for its customers through the institution on a fully-disclosed basis.

An institution also has a customer relationship with consumers if it regularly effects or engages in securities transactions with or for them even if the institution does not hold any of their assets. There is also a customer relationship with a consumer who holds an investment product through the firm, such as when the firm acts as a custodian for securities of for assets in an IRA.

However, consumers who do not establish accounts with a financial institution do not have continuing relationships if the institution provides brokerage services to them on a one-time basis as an accommodation or to liquidate securities without the expectation of engaging in other transactions.

The examples also clarify that consumers will have a customer relationship with an investment company whose shares they own in their own names, even if they purchased those shares through a broker or an investment adviser. In that case, they would be customers of both the broker or adviser who sold the shares *and* of the investment company.

The SEC rules do not apply to the provision of insurance by brokers, funds, and advisers. A variable annuity or variable life insurance contract is, however, both an insurance product and a security. The rules include an example of purchasing a variable annuity as being one situation in which a customer relationship is formed. In this case, the person obtaining a financial product or service from the financial institution is the person purchasing the annuity.

Under the rules, a financial institution will be considered to have established a customer relationship with any individual to whom it makes a loan. If the institution transfers the servicing rights of the loan to another institution, the second institution will establish a customer relationship with the individual and the first institution's customer relationship will end. The originating lender will then have a consumer relationship with the borrower.

However, if the originating lender sells the loan but continues to service the loan, it will continue to have a customer relationship with the borrower, and the purchaser of the loan will have a consumer relationship with the borrower. In those circumstances, the borrower will be entitled to receive initial and annual notices from the loan servicer.

For example, a brokerage firm that buys a loan, but not the servicing rights to the loan, will have a consumer relationship but not a customer relationship with the borrower. The SEC also noted that a brokerage firm purchasing loans for securitization would have to provide notice and opt out to borrowers before sharing their nonpublic personal information with third parties unless the sharing was necessary to effect or administer the securitization.

Because the Gramm-Leach-Bliley Act requires annual notices of the financial institution's privacy policies to its customers, the SEC has interpreted the Act to require more than isolated transactions between an institution and a consumer in order to establish a customer relationship, unless it is reasonable to expect further contact about that transaction between the institution and consumer afterwards. Thus, the rules contemplate that a customer relationship will be one of a continuing nature. This would include a brokerage account or an investment advisory relationship.

Wrap accounts

Examples of a customer relationship include an individual who has an advisory contract with an investment adviser. Similarly, a client who has a written contract with a wrap account sponsor, but not with the wrap account's investment adviser, has a customer relationship with the investment adviser.

Wrap accounts provide investors with a number of investment services for a single "wrap" fee. In a 1992 no-action letter, *Regulatory Services, Inc.*, the staff advised that, for purposes of the brochure delivery rule under the Investment Advisers Act, a contractual relationship exists between a wrap account client and the portfolio manager, even in the absence of a written contract. Reasoning that the same analysis applies under the privacy rules, the SEC believes that a wrap account client has a customer relationship with the portfolio manager.

It may be unclear when the customer relationship with the portfolio manager is established in a wrap account and, therefore, when the portfolio manager must provide the initial notice to the customer. Regulation S-P provides that a customer relationship is established when the consumer enters into a contract with the adviser.

In the 1992 no-action letter, the staff found that the contractual relationship arose no later than the time the portfolio manager began to provide services to the client. Again reasoning by analogy for purposes of the privacy rules, the SEC maintains that a portfolio manager must provide an initial privacy notice to a wrap account client no later than when it begins to provide services to the client.

Advisers to pension plans

An investment adviser that has only institutional clients, including pension plans, does not have customers to whom it must provide privacy notices. While SEC rules do require an investment adviser to provide privacy notices to its customers and consumers, under the rules a consumer or customer must be an individual. Therefore a client that is not an individual, such as a pension plan, is neither a consumer nor a customer of the adviser.

Similarly, beneficiaries of a pension plan that is the adviser's client would not be the adviser's customers. But note that any individual accommodation clients to whom the adviser provides personal financial services would be the adviser's customers for purposes of the privacy rules.

Mutual fund investors

Individuals who purchase mutual fund shares through a broker-dealer are customers of the fund so long as they own the shares in their own names. This is true even if the fund has no direct contact with the individuals. Examples in Regulation S-P provide that an individual who is the record holder of fund shares is the fund's customer. If the broker-dealer is the record holder of fund shares for the benefit of the individual, however, the individual would not be a fund customer.

Also note that a fund may receive nonpublic personal information about a beneficial shareholder from a broker-dealer under exceptions contained in Rules 248.14 or 248.15, for example, to provide tax information directly to the shareholder, without establishing a customer relationship with the shareholder. A fund receiving such nonpublic personal information about a shareholder is also limited in the ways in which it can share or use that information under Rule 248.11(a).

One-time transactions

The SEC has said that a one-time transaction may be enough to establish a customer relationship depending on the nature of the transaction. But a consumer would not become a customer simply by engaging in an isolated transaction that by itself would be insufficient to establish a customer relationship, such as opening a brokerage account solely for the purpose of liquidating or purchasing securities as an accommodation on a one-time basis without the expectation of engaging in other transactions.

Note that the individual in the example would be a consumer for the broker's purposes, requiring the broker to provide notices if it intends to disclose nonpublic personal information about the consumer to non-affiliated third parties.

The SEC recognizes that the distinction between consumers and customers will sometimes require a financial institution to make a judgment about whether a customer relationship is established. When an individual engages in a transaction and is not likely to expect further communication about that transaction from the financial institution, such as brokerage services as an accommodation, a customer relationship will not have been established .

In other situations when a consumer typically would receive some measure of continued service following or in connection with a transaction, such as opening a brokerage account, being the record owner of fund shares, or obtaining investment advice, a customer relationship is established.

Financial Product or Service

A "financial product or service" is a product or service that a financial institution could offer as an activity that is financial in nature, or incidental to such a financial activity, under Section 4(k) of the Bank Holding Company Act (Rule 248.3(o)(1), at ¶ 203). An activity that is complementary to a financial activity, as described in Section 4(k), is not included in the definition of financial product or service.

The definition includes the financial institution's evaluation of information collected in connection with an application by a consumer for a financial product or service even if the application is ultimately rejected or withdrawn. It also includes the distribution of information about a consumer for the purpose of assisting the consumer in obtaining a financial product or service. To avoid confusion as to whether an investment company shareholder is an owner or a customer of the institution, the definition clarifies that the term financial product includes shares of an investment company.

Nonpublic Personal Information

"Nonpublic personal information" is defined by Gramm-Leach-Bliley to mean personally identifiable financial information that is provided by a consumer to a financial institution, results from any transaction with the consumer or any service performed for the consumer, or is otherwise obtained by the financial institution.

The definition also includes any list, description, or other grouping of consumers, and publicly available information pertaining to them, that is derived using any nonpublic personal information. The Act excludes publicly available information as well as any list, description, or other grouping of consumers that is derived without using nonpublic personal information.

Tracking the Act, the SEC rules define "nonpublic personal information" to mean personally identifiable financial information and any list, description or other grouping of consumers that is derived using any personally identifiable financial information that is not publicly available information (Rule 248.3(t)(1), at ¶ 203).

Information will be deemed "publicly available" and thus excluded from the definition of "nonpublic personal information" if a broker, fund, or adviser reasonably believes that the information is lawfully made available to the general public from government records, widely distributed media, or public disclosures required by law.

SEC examples clarify when a firm has a reasonable belief that information is lawfully made publicly available. A firm would have a reasonable belief if it has confirmed, or the consumer has represented, that the information is publicly available from a public source or the firm has taken steps to submit the information to a keeper of government records who is required to make the information publicly available.

The examples also state that a firm would have a reasonable belief that a telephone number is publicly available if the firm located the number in a telephone book or if the consumer told the firm that the number was unlisted. Moreover, the examples clarify that an institution may not assume information about a particular consumer is publicly available simply because that type of information is normally provided to a government recordkeeper and made publicly available by the recordkeeper, because the consumer may have the ability to keep that information nonpublic or to screen his or her identity, such as where the consumer may record a deed in the name of a blind trust.

The SEC rules are based on the underlying principle that, in many circumstances, consumers can control the public availability or identification of their information and that a financial institution should not assume that the information about them is in fact publicly available. Thus, even though a lender typically enters a mortgage in public records to protect its security interest, when borrowers can maintain the privacy of their personal information by owning the property and obtaining the loan through a separate entity, the customer's name would not appear in the public record.

In the case of a telephone number, persons may request that their numbers be unlisted. Therefore, in evaluating if it is reasonable to believe that information is publicly available, a financial institution must decide if consumers have kept the information or their identity from being a matter of public record.

To implement the Act's complex definition of nonpublic personal information, the SEC rules adopt a definition generally consisting of personally identifiable financial information, plus a consumer list or description or grouping of consumers, and publicly available information pertaining to the consumers, that is derived using any personally identifiable financial information that is not publicly available information.

From that body of information, the rules exclude publicly available information, except if the information is disclosed in a manner indicating that the individual is the firm's consumer, and any consumer list derived without using personally identifiable financial information that is not publicly available information.

The rules give examples of how the above definition applies in the context of consumer lists. Nonpublic personal information includes any list of individuals' names and street addresses derived using personally identifiable financial information that is not publicly available, such as account numbers.

However, nonpublic personal information does not include any list of individuals' names and addresses containing only publicly available information, is not derived using personally identifiable financial information that is not publicly available information, and is not disclosed in a manner indicating that any of the individuals on the list is a consumer of a financial institution.

Personally Identifiable Financial Information

The rules define "personally identifiable financial information" to include three categories of information (Rule 248.3(u)(1), at ¶ 203). The first category includes any information that a consumer provides to a financial institution in order to obtain a financial product or service. This would include information provided when opening a brokerage account, entering into an investment advisory contract, or obtaining a margin loan or a financial plan.

For example, if a consumer provides medical information on an application to obtain a financial product or service, such as a variable life insurance contract offered by an insurance company separate account, that information would be considered personally identifiable financial information. Similarly, information that may be required for financial planning purposes, including details about retirement and family obligations, such as the care of a disabled child, would be personally identifiable financial information.

The second category would include any information about a consumer resulting from any transaction between the consumer and the financial institution involving a financial product or service. This would include information about account balance, payment or overdraft history, credit or debit card purchases, securities positions, or financial products purchased or sold.

The third category includes any financial information about a consumer otherwise obtained by the institution in connection with providing a financial product or service. This would include information obtained from a consumer report or from an outside source to verify information a consumer provides on an application to obtain a financial product or service. It would not, however, include information that is publicly available, unless the information is part of a list of consumers that is derived using personally identifiable financial information.

The SEC has clarified that personally identifiable financial information does not include a list of names and addresses of people who are customers of an entity that is not a financial institution. Thus, the names and addresses of people who subscribe to a particular magazine would fall outside the definition.

Under the examples listed in the rules, personally identifiable financial information includes:

- Consumer information provided on an application to obtain a loan, credit card, or other financial product or service;

- Account balance information, payment history, overdraft history, and credit or debit card purchase information;

- The fact that an individual is or has been a customer of the financial institution or has obtained a product or service from the institution. Although some commenters argued that customer relationships should not be considered personally identifiable financial information, the SEC maintained that this information identifies the individual as a customer of the institution and reveals a financial relationship and the receipt of products or services from the institution;

- Any information about the consumer disclosed in a manner indicating that the individual is or has been the firm's consumer;

- Any information that a consumer provides to the firm or that the firm or its agent otherwise obtain in connection with collecting on a loan or servicing a loan;

- Any information the institution collects through an information collecting device from a web server, known as a "cookie";

- Information from a consumer report (Rule 248.3(u)(2), at ¶ 203).

Personally identifiable financial information does not include a list of names and addresses of customers of an entity that is not a financial institution or information that does not identify a consumer, such as aggregate information or blind data that does not contain personal identifiers such as account numbers, names, and addresses.

Despite objections to the broad sweep of the definition, the SEC holds to the reasoning that it is appropriate to treat any information as "financial" if a financial institution obtains it in order to provide a financial product or service. The Commission believes this approach is consistent with the Gramm-Leach-Bliley Act, which, while it does not define "financial," does broadly define financial institution to encompass a large number of entities that engage in activities not traditionally considered financial, such as travel agencies and data processors.

Consequently, the range of information with a bearing on the terms and availability of a financial product or service, or that an institution uses in connection with providing such, is extremely broad and may include medical information and other types of information that may not commonly be thought of as financial.

It includes information a brokerage firm, a mutual fund, or an adviser requests from the consumer, obtains from a transaction involving a financial product or service with the consumer, or otherwise obtains in connection with providing a financial product or service to a consumer. Thus, the information included in the definition of "financial" is data the firm has determined to be relevant in providing a financial product or service.

While sensitive to the need for ready access to identifying information to locate individuals trying to evade their financial obligations, a concern expressed by commenters, the SEC emphasized that names, addresses and phone numbers represent financial information covered by the Act. Brokers, funds, and advisers rely on a broad range of information, including addresses and phone numbers, when providing financial products and services. They use location information to provide a wide variety of financial services, such as sending account statements and disbursing funds to a consumer.

The SEC concluded that it would be improper to exclude some items of information from the definition of personally identifiable financial information simply because a particular firm might not rely on those items when providing a financial product or service.

The Commission noted that names, addresses, and phone numbers, if publicly available, will not be subject to the opt-out provisions unless that information is derivative, that is information that is part of a list, description, or other consumer grouping derived from personally identifiable financial information that is not publicly available information.

An investment adviser's client list is an example of this type of information, even if the list includes clients' names, addresses and phone numbers that are otherwise publicly available. When a consumer does not opt out, a financial institution may disclose nonpublic personal information about a consumer to a nonaffiliated third party if the disclosure is consistent with the firm's opt-out and privacy notices.

Publicly Available Information

The term "publicly available information" means information that the financial institution reasonably believes is lawfully made available to the general public from three broad types of sources (Rule 248.3(v)(1), at ¶ 203). First, information from official public records, such as real estate recordations or security interest filings. Second, information from widely distributed media, such as telephone books, radio programs, or newspapers. Third, information from disclosure required to be publicly made by federal, state or local law, such as securities disclosure documents.

SEC examples clarify when a firm has a reasonable belief that information is lawfully made publicly available (Rule 248.3(v)(2), at ¶ 203). For instance, a firm would have a reasonable belief if it has confirmed, or the consumer has represented, that the information is publicly available from a public source or the firm has taken steps to submit the information to a keeper of government records who is required to make the information publicly available.

The examples also state that a firm would have a reasonable belief that a telephone number is publicly available if the firm located the number in a telephone book or if the consumer told the firm that the number was unlisted. Moreover, the examples clarify that an institution may not assume information about a particular consumer is publicly available simply because that type of information is normally provided to a government recordkeeper and made publicly available by the recordkeeper, because the consumer may have the ability to keep that information nonpublic or to screen his or her identity, such as where the consumer may record a deed in the name of a blind trust.

The SEC has clarified that publicly available information in government records includes information in government real estate records and security interest filings. Publicly available information from widely distributed media includes information from a phone book, a television, or radio program, a newspaper, or a web site that is available to the general public on an unrestricted basis. A web site is not restricted merely because an Internet service provider or a site operator requires a fee or a password, so long as access is publicly available.

As originally proposed, the privacy rules excluded from the definition of publicly available information data obtained over the Internet by using a password or complying with a similar restriction. Commenters maintained that it would be more appropriate to focus on whether the information was lawfully placed on the Internet.

Agreeing with that sentiment, the SEC removed the reference to passwords or similar restrictions from the example of the Internet as a "widely distributed" medium of communication and substituted a standard requiring the information, from the Internet or otherwise, to be available on an unrestricted basis.

Information that an individual specifically asks be compiled, such as information that a locator service provides that may combine confidential information in addition to public information, will not be considered to be available to the general public on an unrestricted basis, regardless of whether the information is provided over the Internet or otherwise.

An Internet site is not restricted merely because a fee or password is required so long as public access is available. One common use of passwords is to confine the access of web site users to specific individual information. However, web site operators may also require user IDs and passwords as a method of tracking access rather than restricting access to the information available through the web site. Internet service providers may charge fees to users to access the site rather than to restrict access to particular data.

Other publicly available sites, such as daily newspapers, may also charge a fee to access archived information. Thus, the definition of "widely distributed media" properly focuses on whether the information is lawfully available to the public rather than on the type of medium from which it is obtained. Conversely, information unlawfully obtained will not be deemed publicly available despite the fact that it may be publicly available through widely distributed media.

Affiliates and Control

The SEC rules incorporate the definition of "affiliate" in the Gramm-Leach-Bliley Act (see Rule 248.3(a), at ¶ 203). Thus, a broker-dealer, investment company or registered investment adviser will be considered to be affiliated with another company if it controls, is controlled by, or is under common control with the other company. The definition includes both financial institutions and entities that are not financial institutions.

The rules also provide that a broker-dealer, investment company, or investment adviser will be considered an affiliate of another company for purposes of the privacy rules if the other company is regulated under Gramm-Leach-Bliley's privacy provisions by one of the federal banking agencies and the privacy rules adopted by the banking agency treat the broker, dealer, investment company, or investment adviser as an affiliate of the other company.

This provision is designed to prevent the disparate treatment of affiliates within a holding company structure. Without this provision, the SEC believes that a broker-dealer in a bank holding company structure might not be considered affiliated with another entity in that organization under the SEC's rules, even though the two entities would be considered affiliated under the privacy rules of the federal banking regulators.

The SEC defines "control" to mean the power to exercise a controlling influence over the management or policies of a company whether through ownership of securities, by contract, or otherwise (Rule 248.3(i), at ¶ 203). In the SEC's view, ownership of more than 25 percent of a company's voting securities will create a presumption of control of the company. This presumption may be rebutted by evidence. In the case of an investment company, however, the presumption will continue until the Commission makes a decision to the contrary according to the procedures described in Section 2(a)(9) of the Investment Company Act.

The definition of "control" is used to determine when companies are affiliated. Under the definition, companies are considered to be affiliates regardless of whether the control is by a company or an individual. The rule limits the presumption of control to ownership of more than 25 percent of the voting securities, consistent with the definition of control in the Investment Company Act.

The SEC emphasized that this definition of "control" does not prevent a finding of control-in-fact in the circumstances that create a presumption of control under the definition in Form BD, the broker-dealer registration form. Form BD defines "control" to mean the power to direct the management or policies of a company, whether through ownership of securities, by contract, or otherwise.

In addition, there is a presumption of control for any person that:

- is a director, general partner, or officer exercising executive responsibility;

- has the right to vote 25 percent or more of a class of voting securities or the power to sell or direct the sale of 25 percent or more of a class of voting securities;

- or, in the case of a partnership, has the right to receive upon dissolution, or has contributed, 25 percent or more of the capital.

Brokers and Dealers

The definition of "broker" simply incorporates the Exchange Act meaning of broker (Rule 248.3(b), at ¶ 203). Although urged to do so, the SEC decided not to exclude foreign banks and thrifts from the definition. While commenters speculated that foreign banks and thrifts will be subject to the privacy rules of the banking regulators, the Commission noted that SEC-registered brokers can include foreign firms that may not be subject to the banking privacy rules, which do not extend to foreign entities that do not have offices in the United States. Similarly, the definition of "dealer" incorporates the definition of dealer in the Exchange Act (Rule 248.3(l), at ¶ 203).

Investment Companies and Advisers

The rules incorporate the definition of "investment company" from the Investment Company Act, whether or not the company is registered with the SEC (Rule 248.3(r), at ¶ 203). Thus, a business development company, which is an investment company but is not required to register with the SEC, is subject to the privacy rules.

The definition of "investment adviser" incorporates the definition under the Investment Advisers Act (Rule 248.3(q), at ¶ 203).

Company

The rules define "company" to mean any corporation, limited liability company, business trust, general or limited partnership, association, or similar organization (Rule 248.3(f), at ¶ 203).

Collect

Gramm-Leach-Bliley requires a financial institution to disclose in its initial and annual notices the categories of nonpublic personal information that the institution collects. Borrowing language from the Privacy Act of 1974, the SEC defines "collect" as obtaining information that the firm organizes or retrieves by the name of the individual or by identifying number, symbol, or other identifying particular assigned to the individual, irrespective of the source of the underlying information (Rule 248.3(d), at ¶ 203).

The method of retrieval is irrelevant to whether information should be protected. Thus, information that is not organized and retrievable in an automated fashion can still be "collected" within the Gramm-Leach-Bliley context. However, information that a brokerage firm, mutual fund, or adviser merely receives and then passes along without retaining a copy would not be "collected" information. This is because the rules require that the information must be organized or retrievable by the financial institution.

Financial Institution

A "financial institution" is defined as any institution the business of which is engaging in activities that are financial in nature, or incidental to such financial activities, as described in Section 4(k) of the Bank Holding Company Act (Rule 248.3(n)(1), at ¶ 203). Gramm-Leach-Bliley also defines "financial institution" and the SEC rules except from the definition those entities that Gramm-Leach-Bliley also excepts.

Although urged to by commenters, the SEC did not exempt debt buyers, securitization trusts, and credit bureaus from the definition. Such exceptions would not be appropriate, said the Commission, because the objectives of the suggested exclusions can be achieved in other ways. Even if a firm is a Gramm-Leach-Bliley financial institution, it will not have any privacy disclosure duties if it does not provide a financial product or service to a consumer.

In most of the situations posited by the commenters, the firm will not meet that test and thus will fall outside the scope of the privacy rules. But note that these firms will still be subject to the limits on reuse and redisclosure under Rule 248.11 with regard to any nonpublic personal information received from a non-affiliated financial institution that has disclosure duties under the privacy rules.

Several commenters asked for clarification on the "financial institution" status of an independent contractor registered representative of a broker-dealer when acting in the capacity of a registered representative. Concluding that the rules adequately cover this situation, the SEC noted that an independent contractor registered representative is, under the Exchange Act, an associated person of a broker-dealer if its activities are subject to the broker-dealer's control, such as when there is a principal agent relationship.

Although a brokerage firm's consumer is not considered a consumer of the firm's agent, an independent contractor may also be an investment adviser who as such acts in a different capacity than as agent for the broker-dealer. In these circumstances, the registered representative is a different financial institution. Thus, an investor obtaining advisory services from a registered representative acting as an investment adviser would be a consumer of the investment adviser.

Federal Functional Regulator

The SEC rules define a "federal functional regulator" as one of the following: (1) Board of Governors of the Federal Reserve System; (2) Office of the Comptroller of the Currency; (3) Board of Directors of the Federal Deposit Insurance Corporation; (4) Director of the Office of Thrift Supervision; (5) National Credit Union Administration Board; and (6) Securities and Exchange Commission (Rule 248.3(m), at ¶ 203).

For purposes of the privacy rules, this term is relevant in determining when an entity is an affiliate and when a broker-dealer, fund, or registered adviser may disclose information to a law enforcement agency. The exception for disclosure as stated in the GLB uses the term "federal functional regulator," which is defined in the statute at Section 509(2) and includes the Secretary of the Treasury for purposes of the exception permitting disclosures to law enforcement agencies.

¶ 104 Initial Privacy Notice

Under Gramm-Leach-Bliley, a financial institution must provide an initial notice of its privacy policies and practices in two circumstances. For customers, the notice must be provided at the time a customer relationship is established. For consumers who do not, or have not yet, become customers, the notice must be provided before disclosing nonpublic personal information about the consumer to a non-affiliated third party.

Tracking the Act, the general SEC rule is that a financial institution must provide a clear and conspicuous notice accurately reflecting the institution's privacy policies and practices to a customer not later than the time when a customer relationship is established and to a consumer before disclosing any nonpublic personal information about the consumer to an unauthorized non-affiliated third party (Rule 248.4(a), at ¶ 204).

The rules as proposed had mandated that the initial notice be provided prior to the time a customer relationship is established. This drew strong protest from commenters, who argued that the Act itself only required the notice at the time a customer relationship is established.

While it did not mandate earlier delivery, the SEC noted that nothing in the rules is intended to discourage a financial institution from providing an individual with a privacy notice at an earlier point in the relationship if the institution wishes to do so in order to help the individual compare its privacy policies with those of other institutions before conducting the transaction.

A financial institution must maintain the protections that the notice represents it will provide. In this regard, the SEC expects that brokers, dealers, investment companies, and investment advisers will take appropriate measures to adhere to their stated privacy policies and practices.

Customer Relationship

For consumers that do not establish a customer relationship, the initial notice must be provided at any point before the financial institution discloses nonpublic personal information to non-affiliated third parties (Rule 248.4(a)(2), at ¶ 204). If the institution does not intend to disclose the information in question or intends to make only those disclosures authorized by one of the exceptions for, among other things, processing and servicing accounts, the institution does not have to provide the initial notice.

The rules identify the time a customer relationship is established as the point at which a financial institution and a consumer enter into a continuing relationship (Rule 248.4(c)(1), at ¶ 204). The examples clarify that, for contractual customer relationships, such as investment advisory relationships, a customer relationship is established when the consumer enters into an oral or written contract that is necessary to conduct the transaction in question.

Thus, a customer relationship is established with a brokerage firm when a consumer executes a securities trade through the firm or opens a brokerage account with the firm. The SEC, however, does not believe that a customer relationship exists when a brokerage firm executes a securities trade for a consumer as an accommodation or to liquidate securities on a one-time basis, for example, when there is no expectation of further transactions.

A consumer who opens an account with an introducing broker establishes a customer relationship with the broker's clearing broker at the same time. Similarly, when a consumer purchases investment company shares and is a record owner of the shares, the consumer establishes a customer relationship with the investment company.

The rule provides special treatment for loans. A financial institution will not have a customer relationship with a consumer if it buys a loan made to the consumer but does not have servicing rights for that loan (Rule 248.4(c)(2), at ¶ 204).

Short-Form Initial Notice

The SEC rules allow a financial institution to provide a short-form initial privacy notice along with an opt-out notice to a consumer with whom the institution does not have a customer relationship (Rule 248.6(d), at ¶ 206). The short-form notice must clearly and conspicuously state that the disclosure containing information about the privacy policies is available on request and provide one or more reasonable means by which the consumer may obtain a copy of the notice.

A firm provides a reasonable means of obtaining the short-form notice if it provides a toll-free number that the consumer may call to request the notice or, for consumers conducting business in person at the firm's office, maintains copies of the notice on hand that can be given to the consumer immediately on request.

The SEC believes the short-form is appropriate because a consumer who does not become a customer of a financial firm may have less interest in some elements of the firm's privacy policies. Thus, the consumer may receive greater benefit from obtaining a short-form notice with the opt-out notice revealing the categories of information the firm may share and the categories of third parties that may receive the information. However, the rules also require that consumers interested in the complete privacy disclosures must be given a reasonable means to obtain them.

Concomitant Notices

The SEC will allow the initial notice to be provided at the same time a financial institution is required to give other notices, such as the requirement that credit terms in margin transactions be disclosed under Exchange Act Rule 10b-16.

Another example of concomitant notice would be the requirement that customers be notified in writing of the existence of a carrying or clearing arrangement for accounts introduced on a fully disclosed basis to another broker under NYSE and NASD rules. Another example would be when an investment adviser provides a client with a written disclosure statement (brochure) not later than the time of entering into an advisory contract with the client.

The SEC intends for this approach to strike a balance between ensuring that customers will receive privacy notices at a meaningful point when establishing a customer relationship and minimizing unnecessary burdens on firms that may result if they are required to provide a consumer with a series of notices at different times in a transaction.

Joint Account Holders

A financial institution is not obligated to provide more than one notice to joint account holders. Accordingly, the rules clarify that one notice may be sent in connection with a joint account. A broker-dealer, fund, or adviser may however, in its discretion, provide notices to each party to the account. This situation might arise, for example, when a financial institution does not want one opt-out election to apply automatically to all joint account holders.

Delivery

The rules require that the initial notice be provided so that each recipient can reasonably be expected to receive actual notice. The notice may be delivered in writing or, if the consumer agrees, electronically. Oral notice is not sufficient. In the case of customers, the notice must be given in a way that the customer may either retain it or access it at a later time.

Delayed delivery

To accommodate a wide range of possible scenarios, the SEC will allow later delivery of the initial notice in appropriate situations. The rules provide three instances when a firm may satisfy the delivery requirements by providing the initial notice within a reasonable time of establishing the customer relationship:

- First, the institution may provide the notice after the fact if the customer has not elected to establish the relationship. This might occur when a brokerage account is transferred to another broker by a trustee selected by the SIPC and appointed by a federal court.

- Second, a broker, fund, or adviser may send a notice after establishing a customer relationship when to do otherwise would substantially delay the customer's transaction and the customer agrees to receive the notice at a later time. An example of this would be when an investor requests over the telephone that a broker execute a securities trade.

- The final exception for delayed delivery is when a non-affiliated broker-dealer or adviser purchases fund shares or establishes a brokerage account on behalf of a customer without the financial institution's prior knowledge.

Having allowed later delivery in some circumstances, the SEC was quick to note that, in most situations, a broker, fund, or adviser should give the initial notice at a point when the consumer still has a meaningful choice about whether to enter into the customer relationship.

The exceptions listed in the examples are not exhaustive, but are intended to illustrate the less frequent situations when delivery would pose a significant impediment to the conduct of a routine business transaction or the consumer agrees to receive the notice later in order to obtain a financial produce immediately.

The delayed notice must be delivered within a reasonable time after the establishment of the customer relationship. Although some commenters urged the mandating of a specific time frame, the Commission declined to do so for two reasons. First, prescribing a maximum number of days would be inappropriate because the circumstances of when after-the-fact notice is proper are likely to vary significantly. Secondly, a rule attempting to accommodate every circumstance is likely to provide more time than is appropriate in many instances.

Mutual Funds

A mutual fund cannot provide the initial privacy notice to a new customer after the customer invests, when it delivers the fund's prospectus and confirmation. The Gramm-Leach-Bliley Act requires a fund to provide an initial notice to customers no later than the time the customer relationship is established.

SEC privacy rules provide that an individual establishes a customer relationship with a fund when the individual purchases fund shares in his or her own name, that is on the trade date. Thus, an initial privacy notice provided with a prospectus and confirmation must be provided to the investor no later than the trade date.

Exceptions to this delivery rule may apply, however, in certain circumstances. A fund may provide the initial privacy notice within a reasonable time after it establishes a customer relationship if:

- Establishing the customer relationship is not at the customer's election;

- Providing notice no later than when the fund establishes a customer relationship would substantially delay the customer's transaction and the customer agrees to receive the notice at a later time; or

- A nonaffiliated broker or dealer establishes a customer relationship between the fund and a consumer without the fund's prior knowledge.

Closed-End Funds

Closed-end funds are subject to the same initial privacy notice delivery requirements as open-end funds (see above). Therefore, if investors buy shares of a closed-end fund that they do not already own through a broker or dealer affiliated with the fund, the fund must provide initial privacy notices to them no later than when the fund establishes the customer relationship, *i.e.*, when the investors purchase fund shares in their own names.

If investors purchase the shares of a closed-end fund that they do not already own through a broker or dealer unaffiliated with the fund, the fund would have a reasonable time to provide an initial notice to them after the customer relationship is established. Under these circumstances, a reasonable time after establishing a customer relationship includes a reasonable time after the fund learns of the customer's purchase of the fund shares. If investors already own shares of the fund, they already will have received an initial privacy notice, and need not receive another initial notice.

Existing Customers

To avoid the burden of providing additional notice to the same existing customers, the rules do not require a firm to give the same customers additional copies of its initial notice every time they obtains a financial product or service so long as the notice most recently provided to them was accurate with regard to the new financial produce or service being purchased (Rule 248.4(d), at ¶ 204).

Mergers

With regard to the merger of two financial institutions or in a takeover situation, the need to provide new initial or opt-out notices to the customers of the acquired entity will depend on whether the notices previously given to them accurately reflect the policies and practices of the surviving institution. If they do, the surviving entity will not have to provide new notices. If the surviving institution does not deliver new notices, it must honor any opt outs the predecessor institution received from customers.

¶ 105 Annual Privacy Notice

Gramm-Leach-Bliley requires a financial institution to provide notice of its privacy policies and practices at least annually to its customers (see Section

503). The rules implement this statute by requiring a clear and conspicuous notice accurately reflecting the current privacy policies and practices to be provided at least once during any 12 consecutive months (Rule 248.5(a)(1), at ¶ 205). The rules governing how to provide an initial notice also apply to annual notices.

In an effort to give flexibility, the rules set forth an example under which a firm may select a calendar year as the 12-month period within which annual notices will be provided and deliver the first annual notice at any point in the calendar year following the year in which the customer relationship was established. A firm must apply the 12-consecutive-month period to its customer consistently,

To implement the Act's requirement that annual notices be provided during the continuation of a customer relationship, the SEC will not make a financial institution provide annual notices to customers with whom it no longer has a continuing relationship (Rule 248.5(b)(1), at ¶ 205).

For example, there would be no continuing relationship if a brokerage account has been closed or an investment advisory contract terminated. In addition, mutual fund shareholders who have redeemed all of their shares, or are determined to be lost security holders would no longer be considered customers of the mutual fund (Rule 248.5(b)(2), at ¶ 205).

The SEC rejected suggestions that it provide the option of a short-form annual notice since Gramm-Leach-Bliley requires a full set of disclosures to each customer once a year. In any event, the notice is neither lengthy nor detailed. Small institutions that do not share information with third parties beyond the statutory exceptions should be able to provide a short streamlined notice. Also, firms can provide annual notices over their web site to a customer who conducts transaction electronically and agrees to electronic disclosure.

¶ 106 Contents of Annual and Initial Notices

The Gramm-Leach-Bliley Act specifies the types of information that financial institutions must include in their initial and annual notices. Section 503(a) sets out the general requirement that a financial institution must provide customers with a notice describing its policies and practices with respect to, among other things, disclosing nonpublic personal information to affiliates and nonaffiliated third parties. Section 503(b) identifies certain elements that must be addressed in that notice.

The required content is the same for both the initial and annual notices of privacy policies and practices. Although the information in the notices must be accurate as of the time the notices are provided, a financial institution may prepare its notices based on current and anticipated policies and practices.

As discussed below, the SEC rules implement Gramm-Leach-Bliley by requiring initial and annual privacy notices to disclose information concerning the following: personal information collected; personal information disclosed; recipients of personal information; information about former customers; disclosures under joint marketing agreements; the right to opt out; disclosures under the Fair Credit Reporting Act; and confidentiality safeguards.

Personal Information Collected

The Act requires a financial institution to tell its customers about the categories of nonpublic personal information that the firm collects. The rules provide an example of how to comply with this requirement that focuses on the source of the information collected. A firm satisfies the requirement to categorize the nonpublic personal information that it collects if it lists the following categories, as applicable:

- Information from the consumer;
- Information about the consumer's transactions with the firm or its affiliates;
- Information about the consumer's transactions with nonaffiliated third parties; and
- Information from a consumer-reporting agency (Rule 248.6(c)(1), at ¶ 206).

Personal Information Disclosed

The Act requires the financial institution to provide information about the categories of nonpublic personal information that may be disclosed. Under Regulation S-P, the SEC's examples of how to comply focus on the content of information to be disclosed. A firm may satisfy this requirement by categorizing information according to source and providing examples of the content of the information (Rule 248.6(c)(2)(i), at ¶ 206).

If a firm reserves the right to disclose all of the nonpublic personal information about consumers that it collects, it may simply state that fact without describing the categories or examples of the nonpublic personal information it discloses (Rule 248.6(c)(2)(ii), at ¶ 206).

A sample clause could state the firm may disclose the following kinds of nonpublic personal information about the consumer:

- Information received on applications or other forms, such as name, address, social security number, assets, and income;
- Information about transactions with the firm, its affiliates, or others, such as account balance, payment history, parties to transactions, and credit card usage; and

- Information received from a consumer reporting agency, such as creditworthiness and credit history.

Recipients of Personal Information

The rules require a disclosure of affiliates and third parties to whom the firm discloses nonpublic personal information (Rule 248.6(a)(3), at ¶ 206). A financial institution will adequately categorize the affiliates and non-affiliated third parties to whom it discloses nonpublic personal information about consumers if it identifies the types of businesses in which they engage. Types of businesses may be generally described, such as financial service providers, non-financial companies, and others, with a few examples to illustrate the types of third parties in each category (Rule 248.6(c)(3), at ¶ 206).

The Act does not require a financial institution to list the categories of persons to whom information may be disclosed under any of the exceptions set out in the rules. The rules state that a financial institution is required only to inform customers that it makes disclosures as permitted by law to non-affiliated third parties in addition to those described in the notice.

The SEC believes that a financial institution, to comply with the requirement that it disclose its policies and practices with respect to sharing information with affiliated and nonaffiliated third parties, must describe the circumstances under which it will share information with affiliates.

Several commenters suggested that the rules should not require that initial and annual notices include categories of affiliates with whom a financial institution shares information. They noted that GLB specifically requires disclosures of categories of nonaffiliated third parties only, and that the only statutorily mandated disclosures concerning affiliate sharing are disclosures required, if any, concerning affiliate sharing under the Fair Credit Reporting Act.

Rejecting this notion, the SEC emphasized that the language and legislative history of GLB Section 503 supports requiring disclosures of affiliate sharing beyond what may be required by the FCRA. Section 503(b) does not state that the items listed in the section are to be the only items set out in a firm's initial and annual disclosures.

Instead, it uses the nonrestrictive phrase "shall include" when discussing the contents of the disclosures, thereby preserving flexibility for the SEC to prescribe rules to require that additional items be addressed in the disclosures consistent with those specifically enumerated.

In addition, Section 503(a) states that the financial institution must provide in its initial and annual notices a clear and conspicuous disclosure of its policies and practices with respect to disclosing nonpublic personal information to affiliates and nonaffiliated third parties, consistent with Section 502, including the categories of information that may be disclosed. While the FCRA disclosures would be a subset of the disclosures required by section 503(a)(1), they may not be sufficient to fully satisfy that requirement.

Finally, the SEC noted that the legislative history of GLB suggests that Congress intended the disclosures to provide more information about affiliate sharing than what may be required under the FCRA. That history underscores the congressional intent of ensuring that individuals have the opportunity to make informed decisions about the privacy policies and practices of financial institutions. Limiting the disclosures about affiliate sharing just to those disclosures that may be required under the FCRA would frustrate that purpose.

Information About Former Customers

GLB Section 502(a)(2) mandates that a financial institution's initial and annual privacy notices must include its policies and practices with regard to disclosing the nonpublic personal information of persons who have ceased to be customers of the institution. Section 503(b)(1)(B) requires that this information be provided with respect to information disclosed to non-affiliated third parties.

The SEC concluded that these sections, taken together, require a financial institution to include in the notices its policies and practices with respect to sharing information about former customers with all affiliates and non-affiliated third parties (Rule 248.6(a)(4), at ¶ 206). However, the rule does not require notice to former customers before sharing nonpublic personal information about them with an affiliate.

But note that an institution intending to share nonpublic personal information about a former customer with a non-affiliated third party would have to provide the customer with notice and opportunity to opt out before sharing the information.

Disclosures under Joint Marketing Agreements

The Act permits a financial institution to disclose a consumer's nonpublic personal information to a non-affiliated third party for the purpose of the third party performing services for the institution, including the marketing of financial products or services under a joint agreement. In this case, a consumer has no right to opt out, but the financial institution must tell the consumer that it will be disclosing the information in question unless the service falls within an exception listed in Gramm-Leach-Bliley Section 502(e).

The rules implement these provisions by requiring that a financial institution disclosing nonpublic personal information to a non-affiliated third party under the joint marketing exception must include in its annual and initial notices a separate description of the categories of information that are disclosed as well as the categories of third parties providing the services (Rule 248.6(a)(5), at ¶ 206).

The examples provide that this mandate can be satisfied by listing the categories of nonpublic information disclosed and stating whether the third party is a service provider performing marketing services on the firm's behalf or on behalf of the firm or another financial institution or a financial institution with which the firm has a joint marketing agreement (Rule 248.6(c)(4), at ¶ 206).

Right to Opt Out

The SEC rules require the initial and annual notices to explain the right to opt out of disclosures of nonpublic personal information to non-affiliated third parties, including the methods available to exercise that right (Rule 248.6(a)(5), at ¶ 206). The Commission's reasoning in mandating this disclosure is that, given that a financial institution's practices with regard to sharing nonpublic personal information with third parties will be affected by the opt-out rights created by the statute, an institution will need to describe these opt-out rights to provide a complete statute-satisfying disclosure.

Disclosures under Fair Credit Reporting Act

Gramm-Leach-Bliley, in Section 503(b)(4), mandates that a financial institution's initial and annual notice include the disclosures required, if any, under Section 603(d)(2)(A)(iii) of the Fair Credit Reporting Act. The SEC rules implement this by requiring that a broker-dealer, fund, or investment adviser's initial and annual notices include any disclosures a financial institution makes under Section 603(d)(2)(A)(iii) of FCRA (Rule 248.6(a)(7), at ¶ 206). To the extent that broker-dealers share information about margin loans, they may be subject to the FCRA.

Some commenters argued that a financial institution should not have to include FCRA disclosures in its annual notices. They noted that GLB Section 506(c) states that nothing in the Act is to be construed to modify, limit, or supersede the operation of the FCRA. These commenters maintained that the "if any" language of Section 503(b)(4), read in the context of Section 506, suggests that, because at most only one notice must be provided under the FCRA, Section 503 should require only one FCRA disclosure under the privacy rules.

Declining the idea, the SEC emphasized that Section 503 does not distinguish between the disclosures to be provided in the initial notice from those to be provided in the annual notice. Thus, Section 503 suggests that any disclosures that are required under the FCRA must be included in both the initial and annual notices.

The SEC interprets the "if any" language in Section 503(b)(4) as an acknowledgment that not all institutions provide FCRA notices because not all institutions engage in the type of affiliate sharing covered by the FCRA. The SEC does not believe that requiring the FCRA notice to appear as part of the annual notice under the privacy rules, modifies, limits, or supersedes the operation of the FCRA.

Financial institutions will have exactly the same FCRA obligations following the effective date of the privacy rules as they had before. The only difference will be that, as required by GLB, a financial institution's initial and annual disclosures about its privacy policy and practices will need to reflect how the institution complies with the affiliate sharing provisions of the FCRA.

Finally, the ability of consumers to opt out of affiliate information sharing under the FCRA affects a financial institution's policies and practices with respect to disclosing information to its affiliates. Failing to include this information and an explanation of how the opt-out right may be exercised would make the disclosures incomplete.

Confidentiality Safeguards

Gramm-Leach-Bliley requires the initial and annual notices to provide information about a financial institution's policies and practices with regard to protecting a consumer's nonpublic personal information. The notices must also include the policies maintained to protect the confidentiality and security of such information. The Act charges the SEC with establishing standards governing the administrative, technical, and physical safeguards of customer information.

Implementing the Act, the SEC rules require a financial institution to place in its annual and initial notices its policies and practices with regard to protecting the confidentiality, security, and integrity of the nonpublic personal information of consumers (Rule 248.6(a)(8), at ¶ 206). A financial institution may comply with the rule as it concerns confidentiality and security if it explains matters such as who has access to the information and the circumstances under which the information may be accessed (Rule 248.6(c)(6), at ¶ 206). The information about integrity should focus on the measures the institution takes to protect against reasonably anticipated threats or hazards.

Although a firm must state whether it has security practices and procedures in place to ensure the confidentiality of the information in accordance with its policies, the firm need not describe technical information about the safeguards used.

Reserving Right to Future Disclosures

A financial institution may place in the privacy notice categories of nonpublic personal information that it reserves the right to disclose in the future (Rule 248.6(e), at ¶ 206). Similarly, the notice can also include categories of affiliates or third parties to whom the institution reserves the right in the future to disclose.

Level of Disclosure Generally

The SEC did not intend to require a brokerage firm, fund, or adviser to publish lengthy disclosures precisely identifying every type of information collected or shared, the name of every entity with which information is shared, and a complete description of the technical specifications of how the firm protects its customer records or the identity of each employee who has access to those records.

Rather, the rules require notices providing consumers with the types of third parties with which a financial institution shares nonpublic personal information, the types of information it shares, and the other information about the firm's privacy policies. In most cases, the initial and annual disclosure requirements can be satisfied by disclosures contained in a tri-fold brochure, the SEC stated.

According to the Commission, a brokerage firm, fund, or adviser need only address those items that apply to the institution. Thus, for example, if an investment adviser does not intend to disclose nonpublic personal information to third parties, it can simply omit any reference to the categories of affiliates and non-affiliated third parties to whom it discloses nonpublic personal information.

¶ 107 Opt-Out Notice

Under Gramm-Leach-Bliley, a financial institution cannot share personal information with a non-affiliated third party unless it: gives a consumer notice of its privacy policies and that the information may be disclosed to a third party; gives the consumer a chance to opt out of that disclosure; and tells the consumer how to exercise the opt-out right.

Under Regulation S-P, the opt-out notices provided by financial institutions must be clear and conspicuous and accurately explain the right to opt out. The notice must tell the consumer that the institution discloses or may disclose nonpublic personal information to non-affiliated third parties, state that a consumer has a right to opt out, and provide a reasonable means by which to do so (Rule 248.7(a)(1), at ¶ 207).

The examples that follow this general rule state that a financial institution will adequately provide notice of the opt-out right if it identifies the categories of nonpublic personal information that may be disclosed and the categories of non-affiliated third parties to whom the information may be disclosed and explains that the consumer may opt out of those disclosures (Rule 248.7(a)(2), at ¶ 207). The firm should also identify the financial products or services that the consumer obtains from the firm to which the opt-out direction would apply.

Inclusion with Initial Notices

A financial institution may provide the opt-out notice together with or on the same written or electronic form as the initial privacy notice. If the firm provides the opt-out notice after the initial notice, the firm must include a copy of the initial notice with the opt-out notice in writing or, if the consumer agrees, electronically (Rule 248.7(c), at ¶ 207).

The SEC does not intend for the opt-out notice to require a more detailed disclosure of categories of nonpublic personal information and non-affiliated third parties than that required in the initial and annual notices. The SEC said that the disclosure in the initial and annual notices on the above categories will suffice for the opt-out notice as well.

Further, if the opt-out notice is part of the same document containing the disclosures that must be included in the initial notice, the firm does not have to restate those disclosures in the opt-out notice. In these circumstances, the rules require only that, when the opt-out and privacy notices are read together, they clearly disclose the categories of nonpublic personal information the firm intends to share and the categories of non-affiliated third parties with whom it will share.

Reasonable Means

The SEC rules require that the opt-out opportunity be reasonable and that the firm honor an opt-out election as soon as reasonably practicable. The rules also state that an opt-out election survives until revoked by the consumer. Such revocation must be in writing or, if the consumer has agreed, electronically.

Under the rules, a firm provides a reasonable means to opt out if it designates check-off boxes in a prominent position on the relevant forms with the opt-out notice, or includes a reply form together with the opt-out notice. A firm could also provide an electronic means to opt out, such as a form that can be sent via electronic mail or a process at the firm's web site, as long as the consumer agrees to electronic delivery. Finally, the firm could provide a toll free number that consumers can call to opt out (Rule 248.7(a)(2)(ii), at ¶ 207).

Conversely, the rules state that a firm may not require consumers to write their own letters in order to opt out. That would not be reasonable. It would also be unreasonable if the only means of opting out as described in any notice after the initial notice is to use a check-off box the firm provided with the initial notice but did not include with the later notice (Rule 248.7(a)(2)(iii), at ¶ 207).

The requirement of a reasonable opportunity to opt out does not mean that a consumer forfeits that right once the opportunity lapses. The SEC concluded that a consumer always has the right to opt out (Rule 248.7(f), at ¶ 207).

Joint Accounts

With regard to joint accounts, a firm has the option of providing one notice per account regardless of the number of persons on the account (Rule 248.7(d), at ¶ 207). However, each account holder must have the right to opt out. The rules also require a firm to state in the opt-out notice provided to a joint account holder whether the firm will consider an opt out by a joint holder as an opt out by all of the account holders or whether each account holder is allowed to opt out separately.

Specific Means and Duration

The rules allow a firm to require that a consumer opt out through a specific means so long as the means is reasonable for the consumer (Rule 248.7(a)(2)(iv), at ¶ 207). The SEC recognizes that a firm may not have systems in place or trained personnel to handle opt-out elections at each point of contact between a consumer and the firm and may thus choose not to honor opt-out elections communicated to the institution through means other than those specified for the consumer.

Commenters expressed concern about the duration of an opt out in situations where a person terminates a relationship and then establishes a relationship several years later. The rules provide that a firm is to treat an opt-out election made by a customer in connection with a prior customer relationship as applying solely to the personal information collected during that relationship.

That opt out will continue until the customer revokes it. However, if the customer relationship terminates and a new one is established at a later point, the firm must then provide a new opt-out notice to the customer in connection with the new relationship and any former opt-out election does not apply to the new relationship.

¶ 108 Revised Privacy Notice

In Rule 248.8 (see ¶ 208), the SEC specifies a financial institution's duties in the event the institution changes its disclosure policies. In that case, a financial institution may not disclose nonpublic personal information to a non-affiliated third party unless the institution first provides a revised notice and a new opportunity to opt out. The institution must wait a reasonable period of time before disclosing information according to the terms of the revised notice in order to give the consumer a reasonable chance to opt out.

Examples in the rule indicate that the revised notice must be provided before the firm discloses: (1) a new category of nonpublic personal information to a third party; (2) nonpublic personal information to a new category of third parties; or (3) nonpublic personal information about a former customer to a third party if the customer has not had the chance to opt out (Rule 248.8(b), at ¶ 208). However, a revised notice is not required if the firm discloses nonpublic personal information to a new third party that was adequately described in the prior notice.

Any revised privacy notice must be delivered in compliance with the general delivery requirements of Rule 248.9 (at ¶ 209).

¶ 109 Means of Delivering Notices

The method of delivering annual, initial and opt-out notices is lumped together in the same rule, but annual notices receive special treatment. The general rule is that a financial institution must provide any privacy or opt-out notices to consumers in a manner that they can reasonably be expected to receive actual notice in writing or, if they agree, electronically (Rule 248.9(a), at ¶ 209).

There is a reasonable expectation that a consumer will receive actual notice if a printed copy is hand delivered to the consumer or mailed to the consumer's last known address. In addition, for consumers and customers who conduct transactions electronically, posting a notice on an Internet web site and requiring them to acknowledge receipt as a step in the process of obtaining a financial product or service is another way of accomplishing delivery (Rule 248.9(b)(1), at ¶ 209).

Responding to suggestions that a financial institution be allowed to deliver initial notices simply by posting them on its web site, the SEC concluded that simply posting the notice on the firm's web site is not sufficient to raise a reasonable expectation that the notice will be received.

With regard to isolated transactions, such as an ATM transaction, the examples provide that the notice should be posted on the ATM screen and the customer required to acknowledge receipt as a necessary step to obtaining the product or service.

A firm cannot provide any privacy notice simply by orally explaining the notice either in person or over the phone (Rule 248.9(d), at ¶ 209).

There is no reasonable expectation that a consumer will receive actual notice of a firm's privacy policies if the firm only posts a sign in its branch or office or generally publishes advertisements of its privacy policy. Similarly, there is no general expectation of notice if the privacy notice is sent by e-mail to a consumer who does not obtain a financial product from the firm electronically.

Annual Notices

Regarding annual notices only, there is a reasonable expectation of receipt if the customer uses the firm's web site to obtain financial products and services and agrees to receive notices at the web site and the firm posts its current privacy notice continuously in a clear and conspicuous manner on the site (Rule 248.9(c)(1), at ¶ 209).

A firm need not send an annual privacy notice to customers who have affirmatively requested no communications from the institution so long as the notice is available on request. However, the firm must provide customers with initial, opt-out and revised notices. Also, firms must provide customers with any communications, such as shareholder reports, required under the federal securities laws.

Householding

Regulation S-P allows a financial institution to deliver a single annual privacy notice to multiple customers who share the same address if the notice is in or accompanies a shareholder report or a prospectus delivered under the SEC's householding rules (Rule 248.9(c)(2), at ¶ 209). The SEC believes that customers whose disclosure documents are already householded would also consent to having their annual privacy notices householded. The same cannot be assumed for other customers.

The Commission currently permits the householding of prospectuses and fund shareholder reports. The privacy rules will allow a broker or fund to consider that customers have actually received an annual privacy notice if such notice is included with a prospectus or shareholder report delivered under conditions set forth in the rules permitting the householding of those documents.

Moreover, a fund can satisfy the annual privacy notice requirement by delivering the notice in or with documents that are delivered to multiple shareholders at the same address even if those documents, such as account statements, are not covered by the householding rules so long as the fund obtained consent to household those types of documents in the manner set forth under the householding rules.

Note that the SEC does not permit broker-dealers, funds, or investment advisers to household initial notices. Householding is limited to annual notices primarily because individuals sharing the same address may not become customers of a firm at the same time. Customers must receive an initial notice no later than when the customer relationship is established, and therefore are likely to receive the initial notice before they have notice of householding.

Similarly, the privacy rules do not permit financial institutions to household opt-out notices. An opt-out notice must provide a reasonable means for the consumer or customer to opt out, and the Commission does not assume that customers whose disclosure documents are householded would consent to householding the means by which they must exercise their right to opt out. For example, a mutual fund required to deliver opt-out notices cannot conduct a household delivery of the opt-out notices.

Retention and Recordkeeping

For customers only, the firm must provide the initial, annual, and any revised notice so that a customer can retain them or obtain them later in writing, or, if agreed, electronically (Rule 248.9(e), at ¶ 209).

The rules provide an example allowing a broker, fund, or adviser to provide only the current privacy notice on a web site to someone seeking to obtain the privacy notice after having received the initial notice. This example responds to a request for clarification concerning potential confusion that might result if the rule required a financial institution to make available every version of its privacy policies.

Records concerning privacy notices delivered to consumers and consumer opt outs must be maintained in accordance with the recordkeeping requirements of the federal securities laws: Exchange Act Rule 17a-4 for broker-dealers; Investment Company Act Rule 31a-2 for funds; and Investment Advisers Act Rule 204-2 for advisers.

Joint Notice

The rules affirm that two or more financial institutions may provide a joint notice so long as it is accurate for each institution (Rule 248.9(f), at ¶ 209). For example, a clearing broker could provide a joint notice with an introducing broker for which it clears transactions on a fully disclosed basis, or a fund complex could provide a joint notice for all the funds in the complex. The SEC emphasized that the notice must be accurate for each institution using it and must identify each institution by name.

A privacy notice provided jointly by multiple financial institutions in a fund complex need not separately name each institution to which the privacy policy applies as long as the notice clearly identifies the financial institutions covered by the privacy policy as members of the fund complex. For example, a privacy policy for the ABC fund complex could state that it applies to all funds that include the ABC name. Conversely, however, if the privacy policy applies to additional funds that do not include the ABC name, the policy should specifically identify those additional funds.

Joint and Multiple Accounts

The rules provide that one notice may be sent in connection with joint accounts (Rule 248.9(g), at ¶ 209). However, a broker, fund, or adviser has the discretion to provide notices to each party to the account. A firm may want to do this if it does not want one opt-out election to apply automatically to all joint account holders.

The privacy rules do not prohibit an institution from providing a single privacy notice to a customer regarding all the customer's accounts. Thus, a mutual fund can deliver to a customer with multiple accounts a single initial or annual privacy notice that applies to all the accounts so long as:

- The privacy notice makes clear each of the accounts to which it applies

- The privacy notice is accurate with respect to the privacy policies applicable to each account, and

- A customer with multiple accounts who receives a single notice can reasonably be expected to receive actual notice in writing with respect to each account.

For example, a customer who receives multiple account statements in a single envelope or who receives a consolidated account statement can reasonably be expected to receive actual notice of a fund's privacy policy that is included in the envelope with the account statements.

¶ 110 Limits on Disclosure to Third Parties

A financial institution cannot share nonpublic personal information with a non-affiliated third party unless: (1) it gives a consumer notice of its privacy policies and that the information may be disclosed to a third party; (2) it gives the consumer a reasonable opportunity to opt out of that disclosure; (3) it tells the consumer how to exercise the opt-out right; and (4) the consumer does not in fact opt out (Rule 248.10(a)(1), at ¶ 210).

The rules define "opt out" to mean a direction by the consumer that the firm not disclose nonpublic personal information about the consumer to a non-affiliated third party.

A key element revolves around the question of when has the consumer had a reasonable opportunity to opt out. Examples in the rules attempt to clarify the concept (Rule 248.10(a)(2), at ¶ 210).

For isolated transactions, such as the provision of brokerage services as an accommodation, the consumer has a reasonable opportunity to opt out if the required notices are provided at the time of the transaction and the consumer is asked to decide, as a necessary part of the transaction, whether to opt out before completing the transaction. In this instance, the broker should not be forced to wait before sharing the information.

For notices provided by mail, however, the SEC thinks that consumers should have additional time. In that situation, it is reasonable to allow consumers to opt out by mailing back a form, by calling a toll-free number, or by any other reasonable means within 30 days after the date the opt-out notice was mailed.

The rules also provide an example of a reasonable opportunity for opting out in connection with electronic accounts. A reasonable opportunity is provided if a customer, having agreed to receive notices electronically, is allowed to opt out by any reasonable means within 30 days after the date that he or she acknowledges receipt of the notices in conjunction with opening the account.

A partial opt out is also permitted by allowing consumers to select certain nonpublic personal information or certain third parties with respect to which they wish to opt out.

¶ 111 Opt-Out Exceptions for Joint Marketing

Gramm-Leach-Bliley Act Section 502(b) creates a joint marketing exception to the opt-out requirement. Under this exception, a firm may disclose specified information to a third party in the performance of marketing the firm's products or other services under a joint agreement. Consumers do not have the right to opt out of disclosing their personal information to nonaffiliated third parties under these circumstances so long as the financial institution satisfies certain requirements.

The exception, which the rules implement, has two statutory conditions. The firm must: (1) fully disclose that it will provide this information to the third party before the information is shared (this disclosure should appear in the initial notice); and (2) contract with the third party to require that the third party will maintain the confidentiality of the information (Rule 248.13(a)(1), at ¶ 213).

The SEC emphasized that this contract should be designed to ensure that the third party will maintain the confidentiality of the information at least to the same extent as is required for the financial institution that discloses it and will use the information solely for the purposes for which the information is disclosed or as otherwise permitted.

The SEC rules define "joint agreement" to mean a written contract pursuant to which the financial institution and one or more financial institutions jointly offer, endorse, or sponsor a product or service.

GLB Section 502(e) contains exceptions allowing financial institutions to share information necessary to allow a third party to perform services for the institution. The SEC believes that, when a financial institution is allowed to share nonpublic personal information with a third party under 502(e), it would not have to first comply with the requirements imposed by 502(b). However, any disclosure to a service provider not covered by 502(e) must satisfy the disclosure and written contract mandates of 502(b).

The SEC believes that the safeguards are sufficient to preclude recipients from sharing a consumer's nonpublic personal information through a chain of third party marketing agreements.

Many commenters asked the SEC to allow financial institutions to grandfather prior joint marketing and servicing agreements or allow institutions to comply with the requirements by notifying existing service providers about the privacy rules. The SEC wants to strike a balance minimizing interference with existing contracts while preventing evasions of the rules. To achieve these goals, the rules provide that contracts entered into by July 1, 2000 must be brought into compliance with the rules by July 1, 2002.

¶ 112 Exceptions for Processing and Servicing Transactions

Gramm-Leach-Bliley, in Section 502(e), creates exceptions to the requirements applying to the disclosure of personal information to non-affiliates for disclosures made in connection with the administration, processing, servicing, and sale of a consumer's account. The SEC rules set out these exceptions, making only stylistic changes to the statutory text.

Under Regulation S-P, the opt-out requirements do not apply if a financial institution discloses nonpublic personal information as necessary to effect, administer, or enforce a transaction requested or authorized by a consumer, or in connection with:

- Processing or servicing a financial product or service requested or authorized by a consumer;
- Maintaining or servicing a consumer's account with the financial institution or with another firm as part of a private label credit card program or other extension of credit on behalf of the firm; or
- A proposed or actual securitization, secondary market sale (including sales of servicing rights), or similar transaction related to the consumer's transaction (Rule 248.14(a), at ¶ 214).

The SEC has defined the phrase "necessary to effect, administer, or enforce a transaction" to mean that the disclosure is: (1) required, or is one of the lawful or appropriate methods, to enforce the institution's rights or the rights of other persons engaged in carrying out the financial transaction or providing the product or service; or (2) required, or is a usual, appropriate, or acceptable method:

- to carry out the transaction or the product or service business of which the transaction is a part, and record, service, or maintain the customer's account in the ordinary course of providing the product or service;

- to administer benefits or claims relating to the transaction or the product or service business of which it is a part;

- to provide a confirmation statement or other record of the transaction, or information on the status or value of the service or product to the consumer or the consumer's agent or broker;

- to accrue or recognize incentives or bonuses associated with the transaction provided by the financial institution or any other party;

- to underwrite insurance at the consumer's request or for reinsurance purposes, or for purposes relating to a consumer's insurance, including preventing fraud, processing claims and payments, and administering benefits;

- in connection with settling a transaction, including the collection of amounts paid, the transfer of receivables, or the audit of payment information (Rule 248.14(b), at ¶ 214).

It should be remembered that these exceptions, as well as the other exceptions covered by Rule 248.15, do not affect a financial institution's duty to provide initial notices of its privacy policies prior to the time it establishes a customer relationship and annual notices thereafter. Those notices must be provided to all customers, even if the institution intends to disclose the personal information only under the servicing and processing exceptions (see proposing release, No. 34-42484 (SEC 2000), 2000 CCH Dec. ¶ 86,242).

Investment Advisers

Under the exceptions, an investment adviser need not provide a customer the opportunity to opt out before sharing nonpublic personal information about the customer with a nonaffiliated broker-dealer in order to execute trades the customer has authorized and a nonaffiliated custodian that holds securities on behalf of the customer.

The investment adviser would not be responsible for the privacy policies of broker-dealers that execute transactions the adviser's clients have authorized. A financial institution is not responsible for the privacy practices of a nonaffiliated third party with whom the institution shares information under an exception listed in Rules 248.14 or 248.15.

In addition, Regulation S-P limits the ability of these nonaffiliates to use and share information they have received in those circumstances. If the nonaffiliate receiving the information under an exception is a registered broker-dealer, fund, or investment adviser, the SEC could enforce the provisions of Regulation S-P with respect to the nonaffiliate.

¶ 113 Other Exceptions to Opt-Out Requirements

Gramm-Leach-Bliley Act Section 502(e) contains other exceptions to the requirements that would otherwise apply to the disclosure of nonpublic personal information to third parties. Rule 248.15 (at ¶ 215) sets out these exceptions for disclosures that are not made in connection with the administration, processing, servicing, or sale of a customer's account, and makes stylistic changes to the statutory language intended to clarify the exceptions.

Consent Exception

One exception to the opt-out requirement implemented by the rules is for disclosures made with the consent or at the direction of the consumer (Rule 248.15(a)(1), at ¶ 215). An example of this would be the consumer consents to having a broker or investment adviser confirm the assets in the consumer's account to a non-affiliated mortgage lender as part of a loan application. In such a situation, consent would allow the financial institution to make the disclosure to the third party without first providing the initial notice or the opt-out notice.

Although urged to place additional consumer safeguards on the consent exception, the SEC declined to do so, noting that the consumer may always revoke the consent. In addition, the SEC emphasized that any financial institution obtaining a consumer's consent to disclose nonpublic personal information should take steps to ensure that the limits of the consent are well understood by both the institution and the consumer.

Other Exceptions

There are other exceptions for information provided to insurance rate advisory organizations, rating agencies, guaranty funds, persons assessing the financial institution's compliance with industry standards, and the institution's own attorneys, accountants, and auditors.

Another exception provides for disclosure of a consumer's personal information to third parties to protect the security of the financial institution's records pertaining to the consumer, product, service, or transaction, or to prevent fraud, or for institutional risk control.

Still another exception allows for resolving customer disputes or inquiries. While another allows personal information to be provided to persons holding a legal or beneficial interest relating to the consumer or to persons acting in a fiduciary or representative capacity on the consumer's behalf.

The SEC rules also provide that the opt-out requirements will not apply to personal information provided to law enforcement agencies, and that includes government regulators and SROs, or provided to comply with federal state, or local laws, or with civil, criminal, or regulatory investigations, or to respond to judicial process or regulators possessing examination and compliance oversight powers.

There is an exception for the disclosure of personal information provided in connection with a sale, merger, transfer, or exchange of all or a portion of a business or operating unit if the disclosure concerns only consumers of the business or unit.

Finally, exceptions are granted for personal information conveyed to a consumer reporting agency in accordance with the Fair Credit Reporting Act or from a consumer report reported by a consumer reporting agency.

¶ 114 Limits on Redisclosure and Reuse

Gramm-Leach-Bliley Act Sections 502(a) and (b) prohibit disclosure to a non-affiliated third party unless the consumer is given an opt-out opportunity and does not opt out. In Section 502(c), the Act limits the redisclosure and reuse of a consumer's nonpublic personal information. Specifically, a non-affiliated third party receiving personal information from a financial institution cannot disclose that information to any person that is not affiliated with either the institution or the third party unless the disclosure would be lawful if made directly by the financial institution (Section 502(c)).

The Act, in Section 502(e), lists a number of general exceptions to the disclosure prohibitions of 502(a) and (b). These general exceptions, which are implemented by Rules 248.14 and 248.15, range from disclosures necessary to servicing and processing an account to that needed to comply with federal or state law.

If a broker, fund, or adviser receives nonpublic personal information provided under Section 502(e) it may disclose the information to its affiliates or to affiliates of the financial institution from which it received the information. The firm may also disclose and use the information under the same type of exceptions in the ordinary course of business to carry out the activity covered by the exception under which the institution received the information. The affiliates may disclose and use the information, but only to the extent permitted the firm.

These same general rules apply to a third party other than a broker, fund, or adviser that receives nonpublic information from a broker, fund, or adviser. Thus, the third party receiving the information under one of the 502(e) exceptions may disclose the information to its affiliates or to the affiliates of the financial institution that made the disclosure. The third party also may disclose and use the information under one of the 502(e) exceptions. The affiliates of the third party may disclose and use the information only to the extent permitted for the third party.

If a broker, fund, or adviser receives nonpublic personal information outside of one of the 502(e) exceptions it may disclose the information to its affiliates, the affiliates of the financial institution that made the initial disclosure, or any other person if the disclosure would be lawful if made directly by the financial institution from which the information was received. Thus, the receiving broker, fund or adviser may disclose under one of the 502(e) exceptions.

If a third party receives information from a financial institution outside the 502(e) exceptions, the third party may disclose to its affiliates or to the affiliates of the institution. The third party also may disclose to any other person if the disclosure would be lawful if made by the financial institution. The third party's affiliates may disclose and use the information to the same extent permitted for the third party.

An entity receiving information outside of a 502(e) exception essentially steps into the shoes of the financial institution that made the initial disclosures. Thus, if the firm made the initial disclosures after representing to its customers that it had carefully screened those to whom it intended to disclose the information, the receiving entity must comply with those representations. Otherwise, the later disclosure by the receiving entity would not comply with the notices given to consumers and would not be lawful.

Even if these representations do not prevent the recipient from redisclosing the information, the recipient's ability to redisclose will be limited by whatever opt-out instructions the consumer gave to the financial institution making the initial disclosures and by any new opt-out instructions the consumer gives after the initial disclosure.

Thus, the receiving entity must have procedures to monitor continually the status of who opts out and to what extent. Given these practical limitations on the ability of a recipient to disclose under another institution's privacy and opt-out notices, entities are most likely to redisclose under one of the 502(e) exceptions.

Third-Party Monitoring

The SEC decided not to impose a specific duty on brokers, funds, and advisers to monitor third parties' use of nonpublic personal information they provide. The rules, however, do not address if obligations to monitor reuse and redisclosure may arise in other contexts. In addition, the limits on reuse in the rules provide basis for an enforcement action to be brought against an entity that violates the limits.

Thus, a financial institution is not responsible under Regulation S-P for the privacy practices of a nonaffiliated third party with whom the institution shares information under an exception listed in Rules 248.14 or 248.15. For example, an investment adviser is not responsible for the privacy policies of broker-dealers that execute transactions the adviser's clients have authorized.

Regulation S-P does limit the ability of these nonaffiliates to use and share information they have received in those circumstances. If the nonaffiliate receiving the information under an exception is a registered broker-dealer, fund, or investment adviser, the SEC could enforce the provisions of Regulation S-P with respect to the nonaffiliate. Another regulator specified in the Gramm-Leach-Bliley Act would enforce the privacy regulations with respect to a nonaffiliated financial institution subject to that regulator's jurisdiction.

¶ 115 Limits on Sharing Account Number Information

Gramm-Leach-Bliley Section 502(d) prohibits a financial institution from disclosing, other than to a consumer reporting agency, account numbers or access codes for a credit card account or deposit account to any non-affiliated third party for use in telemarketing or direct mail or electronic marketing. SEC Rule 248.12 (at ¶ 212) tracks this statutory prohibition. The rule also contains two exceptions.

One exception allows a financial institution to disclose account numbers to an agent for the purpose of marketing the institution's financial product or services as long as the agent is not authorized to initiate charges to the account (Rule 248.12(b)(1), at ¶ 212). While a financial institution will frequently use agents to assist it in marketing its products, the SEC feared that providing agents access to a consumer's account number may erode a consumer's protections.

A second exception provides that account numbers could be disclosed to a participant in a private label credit card program or an affinity or similar program when the program participants are identified to the customer when the customer enters the program (Rule 248.12(b)(2), at ¶ 212).

Although the prohibition on disclosure of account numbers apparently has no exceptions in the statute, the House-Senate conference said that, in exercising their authority under Section 504(b) to grant exceptions, the agencies may consider it consistent with the purposes of the privacy code to allow the disclosure of customer account numbers or access codes in an encrypted, scrambled, or similarly coded form when the disclosure is authorized by the customer and is necessary to service or process a transaction expressly requested or authorized by the customer.

Commenters urged the SEC to use its exemptive authority to allow the transmission of account numbers in encrypted form. The SEC believes that an encrypted account number without the key is not the same as the number itself and thus falls outside the prohibition in Section 502(d). The Act focuses on numbers that provide access to an account.

The encrypted number, however, operates as an identifier attached to an account for internal tracking purposes only, and without the key does not allow someone to access an account. For this reason, the rule clarifies that an account number or similar form of access number or code does not include a number or code in an encrypted number form so long as the financial institution does not give the recipient the means to decrypt the number.

¶ 116 Fair Credit Reporting Act

Gramm-Leach-Bliley provides that its privacy provisions should not be construed to modify, limit, or supersede the operation of the Fair Credit Reporting Act. Further, no inference is to be drawn on the basis of the privacy provisions whether information is transaction or experience information under FCRA Section 603. Rule 248.16 (at ¶ 216) restates Gramm-Leach-Bliley, making only minor clarifying changes.

¶ 117 State Laws

Under Section 507 of the Gramm-Leach-Bliley Act, state laws providing greater privacy protections are not preempted. Determinations of whether a state law provides greater protections than the Act are to be made by the Federal Trade Commission after consultation with the agency that regulates either the party filing a complaint or the financial institution about whom the complaint was filed. The SEC rules essentially restate Section 507, noting that the rules do not preempt state laws providing greater consumer protection (Rule 248.17, at ¶ 217).

¶ 118 Privacy Protection Standards

Gramm-Leach-Bliley directs the SEC to establish appropriate standards for financial institutions relating to administrative, technical, and physical safeguards to protect customer records and information. The rules implement this statutory mandate by requiring every broker-dealer, fund, and adviser to adopt policies and procedures to address these safeguards (Rule 248.30, at ¶ 219). The rules further require that the policies and procedures be reasonably designed to insure the security and confidentiality of customer information, protect against anticipated threats to the security or integrity of customer information, and protect against unauthorized access to or use of customer records or information that could result in substantial harm or inconvenience to any customer.

The SEC decided not to prescribe specific procedures or policies that a financial institution must adopt. Rather, the Commission believes it more appropriate for each institution to tailor its policies and procedures to its own systems of information gathering and transfer and the needs of its own customers.

Strongly supporting what it called the SEC's "flexible, process-based approach," the Investment Company Institute said that the approach will ensure that every fund complex has appropriate procedures in place to ensure the integrity, confidentiality, and security of customer information while allowing them to properly tailor and amend those procedures.

¶ 119 Guidance for Certain Entities

In adopting Regulation S-P, the Commission issued specific guidance for certain entities subject to the rules (see Release No. 34-42974 (SEC 2000), Part VI., 2000 CCH Dec. ¶ 86,313). This guidance, used in conjunction with the sample clauses in the appendix (see ¶ 220), attempts to minimize the burden and costs to specified broker-dealers, funds, and registered advisers. These entities, according to the SEC, generally need not provide an opt-out notice or opt-out rights to their customers. In short, initial and annual privacy notices will suffice.

Covered Entities

This guidance applies only to certain financial institutions, *i.e.*, those whose disclosures of personal information to unaffiliated third parties are exempt under Regulation S-P. Specifically, the SEC's advice covers those entities that:

- Do not have any affiliates;
- Only disclose nonpublic personal information to nonaffiliated third parties in accordance with an exception under Rules 248.14 or 248.15, such as in connection with servicing or processing a financial product or service that a consumer requests or authorizes; and
- Do not reserve the right to disclose nonpublic personal information to nonaffiliated third parties, except under Rules 248.14 and 248.15.

In general, if a covered entity discloses nonpublic personal information to nonaffiliated third parties only as authorized under an exception, then its only duties under Regulation S-P are to provide initial and annual privacy notices to each of its customers. The institution need not provide an opt-out notice or opt-out rights to its customers.

Initial Notice

Covered entities must provide an initial notice to each of their customers. A "customer" is a natural person who has a continuing relationship with the entity, as described in Rule 248.4(c) (at ¶ 204). In general, an individual who opens a brokerage account or enters into an investment advisory contract (whether written or oral) with a financial institution is its customer. By contrast, an individual who establishes an account solely for the purpose of liquidating or purchasing securities as an accommodation, *i.e.*, on a one-time basis, without the expectation of engaging in other transactions, is not a customer. In other words, the entity must provide initial and annual notices to each of its customers, but not to others.

Time of Delivery

A covered entity must provide an initial privacy notice to each of its customers when or before it establishes a customer relationship (Rule 248.4(a)(1), at ¶ 204). For example, the entity must provide a privacy notice to an individual not later than when that individual opens a brokerage account or purchases fund shares in his or her own name. Thus, the entity can provide the notice to a brokerage account customer together with the account agreement or to a fund shareholder with the application to purchase shares.

If an existing customer obtains a new financial product or service from the entity, then the entity need not provide another initial notice to that customer (Rule 248.4(d), at ¶ 204) if the earlier notice covered the subsequent product.

> *Example*—If Alison Individual walks into Broker-Dealer for the first time on July 2, 2001, to open a cash account, then Broker-Dealer complies with Rule 248.4(a)(1) of the rules if it provides an initial notice to Alison together with the account agreement. When Alison opens her cash account, she becomes a customer of Broker-Dealer. Alison maintains her cash account and, six months later, returns to the Broker-Dealer to open a margin account. If the initial notice that the Broker-Dealer provided to Alison was accurate with respect to the margin account, then the Broker-Dealer need not provide another initial notice to her when she opens the margin account because it has provided a notice to Alison that covered the margin account when she opened her cash account.

Delivery Method

A covered entity must provide its initial notice so that each customer can reasonably be expected to receive it (Rule 248.9(a), at ¶ 209). For example, the entity may provide the initial notice by mailing a printed copy of it together with a prospectus. Hand-delivering a printed copy of the notice to the customer together with a brokerage account application or an investment advisory contract will also suffice. If two or more customers jointly obtain a financial product or service, the entity may provide one initial notice to those customers jointly.

Annual Notice

During the continuation of the customer relationship, covered entities must provide an annual notice to the customer, as described in Rule 248.5(a) (at ¶ 205). The entity must provide an annual notice to each customer at least once in any period of 12 consecutive months during which the customer relationship exists. The entity may define the 12-month period, but must consistently apply that period to the customer. It may define the 12-month period as a calendar year and provide the annual notice to the customer once in each calendar year following the calendar year in which it provided the initial notice. The entity need not provide an annual notice in addition to an initial notice in the same 12-month period.

> *Example*—Assume that Broker-Dealer defines the 12-consecutive-month period as a calendar year and provides annual notices to all of its customers on October 1 of each year. If Alison Individual opens a cash account with Broker-Dealer on July 2, 2001, thereby becoming a customer, then Broker-Dealer must provide an initial notice to Alison together with the account agreement or earlier. Broker-Dealer must provide an annual notice to Alison by December 31, 2002. If Broker-Dealer provides an annual notice to Alison on October 1, 2002, as it does for other customers, then it must provide the next annual notice to Alison not later than October 1, 2003.

Delivery Method

Like the initial notice, a financial institution must provide the annual notice so that each customer can reasonably be expected to receive actual notice of it, in writing (Rule 248.9(a), at ¶ 209). Mailing a printed copy of the notice to the customer's last known address will suffice. If two or more customers jointly obtain a financial product or service, the institution may provide one annual notice to those customers jointly (Rule 248.9(g), at ¶ 209).

Contents of Both Notices

The SEC's guidance also addresses the contents of the initial and annual notices. Under Regulation S-P, both the initial and annual notices must include an accurate description of:

- The categories of nonpublic personal information collected (Rule 248.6(a)(1));
- The fact that the institution does not disclose nonpublic personal information about its current and former customers to affiliates or nonaffiliated third parties, except as authorized by Rules 248.14 and 248.15 (Rule 248.6(a)(2)-(4), at ¶ 206). When describing the categories with

respect to those parties, the institution need only state that it makes disclosures to other nonaffiliated third parties as permitted by law (Rule 248.6(c));

- The institution's policies and practices as to protecting the confidentiality and security of nonpublic personal information (Rule 248.6(a)(8), at ¶ 206).

For each item above, the institution may use a sample clause from the Appendix, provided that the clause accurately describes the institution's actual policies and practices. Both the initial and annual notices must be clear and conspicuous, as defined in Rule 248.3(c) (at ¶ 203).

Example

If Broker-Dealer (i) does not have any affiliates and (ii) only discloses nonpublic personal information to nonaffiliated third parties as authorized under Rules 248.14 and 248.15, Broker-Dealer may comply with the requirements of Rule 248.6 by using the following notice, if applicable:

> *Broker-Dealer collects nonpublic personal information about you from the following sources:*
>
> - *Information we receive from you on applications or other forms;*
> - *Information about your transactions with us or others; and*
> - *Information we receive from a consumer reporting agency.*
>
> *We do not disclose any nonpublic personal information about you to anyone, except as permitted by law.*
>
> *If you decide to close your account(s) or become an inactive customer, we will adhere to the privacy policies and practices as described in this notice.*
>
> *Broker-Dealer restricts access to your personal and account information to those employees who need to know that information to provide products or services to you. Broker-Dealer maintains physical, electronic, and procedural safeguards to guard your nonpublic personal information.*

The Commission notes that financial institutions need only describe those general categories that apply to their policies and practices. Thus, a broker-dealer that does not collect information from a "consumer reporting agency," for example, need not describe that category in the notice, as indicated above.

Disclosure to Service Providers, Joint Marketers

The SEC guidance also covers the disclosure of personal information to service providers and joint marketers. If a covered entity discloses nonpublic personal information in accordance with the exception in Rule 248.13 (for service providers and joint marketers), it also must include an accurate description of that information. The entity may comply with Rule 248.13 by including the following sample clause, if applicable, in the example described above:

> *We may disclose all of the information we collect, as described [describe location in the notice, such as "above" or "below"] to companies that perform marketing services on our behalf or to other financial institutions with whom we have joint marketing agreements.*

Internal Controls, Supervision

The Commission expects brokers-dealers, funds, and registered advisers to create appropriate internal control systems and exercise appropriate supervision over compliance with Regulation S-P. Compliance systems could include the maintenance of copies of the notices provided to consumers and customers, documentation in customer files showing compliance, and procedures for handling and monitoring opt-out requests.

APPENDIX—REGULATION S-P

17 CFR Part 248

[¶ 201] Purpose and Scope

§ 248.1. (a) *Purpose.* This part governs the treatment of nonpublic personal information about consumers by the financial institutions listed in paragraph (b) of this section. This part:

(1) Requires a financial institution to provide notice to customers about its privacy policies and practices;

(2) Describes the conditions under which a financial institution may disclose nonpublic personal information about consumers to nonaffiliated third parties; and

(3) Provides a method for consumers to prevent a financial institution from disclosing that information to most nonaffiliated third parties by "opting out" of that disclosure, subject to the exceptions in § § 248.13, 248.14, and 248.15.

(b) *Scope.* This part applies only to nonpublic personal information about individuals who obtain financial products or services primarily for personal, family, or household purposes from the institutions listed below. This part does not apply to information about companies or about individuals who obtain financial products or services primarily for business, commercial, or agricultural purposes. This part applies to brokers, dealers, and investment companies, as well as to investment advisers that are registered with the Commission. It also applies to foreign (non-resident) brokers, dealers, investment companies and investment advisers that are registered with the Commission. These entities are referred to in this part as "you." This part does not apply to foreign (non-resident) brokers, dealers, investment companies and investment advisers that are not registered with the Commission. Nothing in this part modifies, limits, or supersedes the standards governing individually identifiable health information promulgated by the Secretary of Health and Human Services under the authority of sections 262 and 264 of the Health Insurance Portability and Accountability Act of 1996 (42 U.S.C. 1320d—1320d-8).

[¶ 202] Rule of Construction

§ 248.2. The examples in this part and the sample clauses in the Appendix of this part provide guidance concerning the rule's application in ordinary circumstances. The facts and circumstances of each individual situation, however, will determine whether compliance with an example or use of a sample clause, to the extent applicable, constitutes compliance with this part.

[¶ 203] Definitions

§ 248.3. As used in this part, unless the context requires otherwise:

(a) *Affiliate* of a broker, dealer, or investment company, or an investment adviser registered with the Commission means any company that controls, is controlled by, or is under common control with the broker, dealer, or investment company, or investment adviser registered with the Commission. In addition, a broker, dealer, or investment company, or an investment adviser registered with the Commission will be deemed an affiliate of a company for purposes of this part if:

(1) That company is regulated under Title V of the G-L-B Act by the Federal Trade Commission or by a Federal functional regulator other than the Commission; and

(2) Rules adopted by the Federal Trade Commission or another federal functional regulator under Title V of the G-L-B Act treat the broker, dealer, or investment company, or investment adviser registered with the Commission as an affiliate of that company.

(b) *Broker* has the same meaning as in section 3(a)(4) of the Securities Exchange Act of 1934 (15 U.S.C. 78c(a)(4)).

(c)(1) *Clear and conspicuous* means that a notice is reasonably understandable and designed to call attention to the nature and significance of the information in the notice.

(2) *Examples.* (i) *Reasonably understandable.* You make your notice reasonably understandable if you:

(A) Present the information in the notice in clear, concise sentences, paragraphs, and sections;

(B) Use short explanatory sentences or bullet lists whenever possible;

(C) Use definite, concrete, everyday words and active voice whenever possible;

(D) Avoid multiple negatives;

(E) Avoid legal and highly technical business terminology whenever possible; and

(F) Avoid explanations that are imprecise and readily subject to different interpretations.

(ii) *Designed to call attention.* You design your notice to call attention to the nature and significance of the information in it if you:

(A) Use a plain-language heading to call attention to the notice;

(B) Use a typeface and type size that are easy to read;

(C) Provide wide margins and ample line spacing;

(D) Use boldface or italics for key words; and

(E) Use distinctive type size, style, and graphic devices, such as shading or sidebars when you combine your notice with other information.

(iii) *Notices on web sites.* If you provide a notice on a web page, you design your notice to call attention to the nature and significance of the information in it if you use text or visual cues to encourage scrolling down the page if necessary to view the entire notice and ensure that other elements on the web site (such as text, graphics, hyperlinks, or sound) do not distract attention from the notice, and you either:

(A) Place the notice on a screen that consumers frequently access, such as a page on which transactions are conducted; or

(B) Place a link on a screen that consumers frequently access, such as a page on which transactions are conducted, that connects directly to the notice and is labeled appropriately to convey the importance, nature, and relevance of the notice.

(d) *Collect* means to obtain information that you organize or can retrieve by the name of an individual or by identifying number, symbol, or other identifying particular assigned to the individual, irrespective of the source of the underlying information.

(e) *Commission* means the Securities and Exchange Commission.

(f) *Company* means any corporation, limited liability company, business trust, general or limited partnership, association, or similar organization.

(g)(1) *Consumer* means an individual who obtains or has obtained a financial product or service from you that is to be used primarily for personal, family, or household purposes, or that individual's legal representative.

(2) *Examples.* (i) An individual is your consumer if he or she provides nonpublic personal information to you in connection with obtaining or seeking to obtain brokerage services or investment advisory services, whether or not you provide brokerage services to the individual or establish a continuing relationship with the individual.

(ii) An individual is not your consumer if he or she provides you only with his or her name, address, and general areas of investment interest in connection with a request for a prospectus, an investment adviser brochure, or other information about financial products or services.

(iii) An individual is not your consumer if he or she has an account with another broker or dealer (the introducing broker-dealer) that carries securities for the individual in a special omnibus account with you (the clearing broker-dealer) in the name of the introducing broker-dealer, and when you receive only the account numbers and transaction information of the introducing broker-dealer's consumers in order to clear transactions.

(iv) If you are an investment company, an individual is not your consumer when the individual purchases an interest in shares you have issued only through a broker or dealer or investment adviser who is the record owner of those shares.

(v) An individual who is a consumer of another financial institution is not your consumer solely because you act as agent for, or provide processing or other services to, that financial institution.

(vi) An individual is not your consumer solely because he or she has designated you as trustee for a trust.

(vii) An individual is not your consumer solely because he or she is a beneficiary of a trust for which you are a trustee.

(viii) An individual is not your consumer solely because he or she is a participant or a beneficiary of an employee benefit plan that you sponsor or for which you act as a trustee or fiduciary.

(h) *Consumer reporting agency* has the same meaning as in section 603(f) of the Fair Credit Reporting Act (15 U.S.C. 1681a(f)).

(i) *Control* of a company means the power to exercise a controlling influence over the management or policies of a company whether through ownership of securities, by contract, or otherwise. Any person who owns beneficially, either directly or through one or more controlled companies, more than 25 percent of the voting securities of any company is presumed to control the company. Any person who does not own more than 25 percent of the voting securities of any company will be presumed not to control the company. Any presumption regarding control may be rebutted by evidence, but, in the case of an investment company, will continue until the Commission makes a decision to the contrary according to the procedures described in section 2(a)(9) of the Investment Company Act of 1940 (15 U.S.C. 80a-2(a)(9)).

(j) *Customer* means a consumer who has a customer relationship with you.

(k)(1) *Customer relationship* means a continuing relationship between a consumer and you under which you provide one or more financial products or services to the consumer that are to be used primarily for personal, family, or household purposes.

(2) *Examples.* (i) *Continuing relationship.* A consumer has a continuing relationship with you if:

(A) The consumer has a brokerage account with you, or if a consumer's account is transferred to you from another broker-dealer;

(B) The consumer has an investment advisory contract with you (whether written or oral);

(C) The consumer is the record owner of securities you have issued if you are an investment company;

(D) The consumer holds an investment product through you, such as when you act as a custodian for securities or for assets in an Individual Retirement Arrangement;

(E) The consumer purchases a variable annuity from you;

(F) The consumer has an account with an introducing broker or dealer that clears transactions with and for its customers through you on a fully disclosed basis;

(G) You hold securities or other assets as collateral for a loan made to the consumer, even if you did not make the loan or do not effect any transactions on behalf of the consumer; or

(H) You regularly effect or engage in securities transactions with or for a consumer even if you do not hold any assets of the consumer.

(ii) *No continuing relationship.* A consumer does not, however, have a continuing relationship with you if you open an account for the consumer solely for the purpose of liquidating or purchasing securities as an accommodation, i.e., on a one time basis, without the expectation of engaging in other transactions.

(l) *Dealer* has the same meaning as in section 3(a)(5) of the Securities Exchange Act of 1934 (15 U.S.C. 78c(a)(5)).

(m) *Federal functional regulator* means:

(1) The Board of Governors of the Federal Reserve System;

(2) The Office of the Comptroller of the Currency;

(3) The Board of Directors of the Federal Deposit Insurance Corporation;

(4) The Director of the Office of Thrift Supervision;

(5) The National Credit Union Administration Board; and

(6) The Securities and Exchange Commission.

(n)(1) *Financial institution* means any institution the business of which is engaging in activities that are financial in nature or incidental to such financial activities as described in section 4(k) of the Bank Holding Company Act of 1956 (12 U.S.C. 1843(k)).

(2) *Financial institution* does not include:

(i) Any person or entity with respect to any financial activity that is subject to the jurisdiction of the Commodity Futures Trading Commission under the Commodity Exchange Act (7 U.S.C. 1 *et seq.*);

(ii) The Federal Agricultural Mortgage Corporation or any entity chartered and operating under the Farm Credit Act of 1971 (12 U.S.C. 2001 *et seq.*); or

(iii) Institutions chartered by Congress specifically to engage in securitizations, secondary market sales (including sales of servicing rights), or similar transactions related to a transaction of a consumer, as long as such institutions do not sell or transfer nonpublic personal information to a nonaffiliated third party.

(o)(1) *Financial product or service* means any product or service that a financial holding company could offer by engaging in an activity that is financial in nature or incidental to such a financial activity under section 4(k) of the Bank Holding Company Act of 1956 (12 U.S.C. 1843(k)).

(2) *Financial service* includes your evaluation or brokerage of information that you collect in connection with a request or an application from a consumer for a financial product or service.

(p) *G-L-B Act* means the Gramm-Leach-Bliley Act (Pub. L. No. 106-102, 113 Stat. 1338 (1999)).

(q) *Investment adviser* has the same meaning as in section 202(a)(11) of the Investment Advisers Act of 1940 (15 U.S.C. 80b-2(a)(11)).

(r) *Investment company* has the same meaning as in section 3 of the Investment Company Act of 1940 (15 U.S.C. 80a-3), and includes a separate series of the investment company.

(s)(1) *Nonaffiliated third party* means any person except:

(i) Your affiliate; or

(ii) A person employed jointly by you and any company that is not your affiliate (but *nonaffiliated third party* includes the other company that jointly employs the person).

(2) *Nonaffiliated third party* includes any company that is an affiliate solely by virtue of your or your affiliate's direct or indirect ownership or control of the company in conducting merchant banking or investment banking activities of the type described in section 4(k)(4)(H) or insurance company investment activities of the type described in section 4(k)(4)(I) of the Bank Holding Company Act (12 U.S.C. §§ 1843(k)(4)(H) and (I)).

(t)(1) *Nonpublic personal information* means:

(i) Personally identifiable financial information; and

(ii) Any list, description, or other grouping of consumers (and publicly available information pertaining to them) that is derived using any personally identifiable financial information that is not publicly available information.

(2) *Nonpublic personal information* does not include:

(i) Publicly available information, except as included on a list described in paragraph (t)(1)(ii) of this section or when the publicly available information is disclosed in a manner that indicates the individual is or has been your consumer; or

(ii) Any list, description, or other grouping of consumers (and publicly available information pertaining to them) that is derived without using any personally identifiable financial information that is not publicly available information.

(3) *Examples of lists.* (i) Nonpublic personal information includes any list of individuals' names and street addresses that is derived in whole or in part using

personally identifiable financial information that is not publicly available information, such as account numbers.

(ii) Nonpublic personal information does not include any list of individuals' names and addresses that contains only publicly available information, is not derived in whole or in part using personally identifiable financial information that is not publicly available information, and is not disclosed in a manner that indicates that any of the individuals on the list is a consumer of a financial institution.

(u)(1) *Personally identifiable financial information* means any information:

(i) A consumer provides to you to obtain a financial product or service from you;

(ii) About a consumer resulting from any transaction involving a financial product or service between you and a consumer; or

(iii) You otherwise obtain about a consumer in connection with providing a financial product or service to that consumer.

(2) *Examples.* (i) *Information included.* Personally identifiable financial information includes:

(A) Information a consumer provides to you on an application to obtain a loan, credit card, or other financial product or service;

(B) Account balance information, payment history, overdraft history, and credit or debit card purchase information;

(C) The fact that an individual is or has been one of your customers or has obtained a financial product or service from you;

(D) Any information about your consumer if it is disclosed in a manner that indicates that the individual is or has been your consumer;

(E) Any information that a consumer provides to you or that you or your agent otherwise obtain in connection with collecting on a loan or servicing a loan;

(F) Any information you collect through an Internet "cookie" (an information collecting device from a web server); and

(G) Information from a consumer report.

(ii) *Information not included.* Personally identifiable financial information does not include:

(A) A list of names and addresses of customers of an entity that is not a financial institution; or

(B) Information that does not identify a consumer, such as aggregate information or blind data that does not contain personal identifiers such as account numbers, names, or addresses.

(v)(1) *Publicly available information* means any information that you reasonably believe is lawfully made available to the general public from:

(i) Federal, State, or local government records;

(ii) Widely distributed media; or

(iii) Disclosures to the general public that are required to be made by federal, State, or local law.

(2) *Examples.* (i) *Reasonable belief.* (A) You have a reasonable belief that information about your consumer is made available to the general public if you have

confirmed, or your consumer has represented to you, that the information is publicly available from a source described in paragraphs (v)(1)(i)—(iii) of this section;

(B) You have a reasonable belief that information about your consumer is made available to the general public if you have taken steps to submit the information, in accordance with your internal procedures and policies and with applicable law, to a keeper of federal, State, or local government records that is required by law to make the information publicly available.

(C) You have a reasonable belief that an individual's telephone number is lawfully made available to the general public if you have located the telephone number in the telephone book or the consumer has informed you that the telephone number is not unlisted.

(D) You do not have a reasonable belief that information about a consumer is publicly available solely because that information would normally be recorded with a keeper of federal, State, or local government records that is required by law to make the information publicly available, if the consumer has the ability in accordance with applicable law to keep that information nonpublic, such as where a consumer may record a deed in the name of a blind trust.

(ii) *Government records.* Publicly available information in government records includes information in government real estate records and security interest filings.

(iii) *Widely distributed media.* Publicly available information from widely distributed media includes information from a telephone book, a television or radio program, a newspaper, or a web site that is available to the general public on an unrestricted basis. A web site is not restricted merely because an Internet service provider or a site operator requires a fee or a password, so long as access is available to the general public.

(w) *You* means:

(1) Any broker or dealer;

(2) Any investment company; and

(3) Any investment adviser registered with the Commission under the Investment Advisers Act of 1940.

Subpart A—Privacy and Opt Out Notices

[¶ 204] Initial Privacy Notice to Consumers Required

§ 248.4. (a) *Initial notice requirement.* You must provide a clear and conspicuous notice that accurately reflects your privacy policies and practices to:

(1) *Customer.* An individual who becomes your customer, not later than when you establish a customer relationship, except as provided in paragraph (e) of this section; and

(2) *Consumer.* A consumer, before you disclose any nonpublic personal information about the consumer to any nonaffiliated third party, if you make such a disclosure other than as authorized by § § 248.14 and 248.15.

(b) *When initial notice to a consumer is not required.* You are not required to provide an initial notice to a consumer under paragraph (a) of this section if:

(1) You do not disclose any nonpublic personal information about the consumer to any nonaffiliated third party, other than as authorized by § § 248.14 and 248.15; and

(2) You do not have a customer relationship with the consumer.

(c) *When you establish a customer relationship.* (1) *General rule.* You establish a customer relationship when you and the consumer enter into a continuing relationship.

(2) *Special rule for loans.* You do not have a customer relationship with a consumer if you buy a loan made to the consumer but do not have the servicing rights for that loan.

(3) *Examples of establishing customer relationship.* You establish a customer relationship when the consumer:

(i) Effects a securities transaction with you or opens a brokerage account with you under your procedures;

(ii) Opens a brokerage account with an introducing broker or dealer that clears transactions with and for its customers through you on a fully disclosed basis;

(iii) Enters into an advisory contract with you (whether in writing or orally); or

(iv) Purchases shares you have issued (and the consumer is the record owner of the shares), if you are an investment company.

(d) *Existing customers.* When an existing customer obtains a new financial product or service from you that is to be used primarily for personal, family, or household purposes, you satisfy the initial notice requirements of paragraph (a) of this section as follows:

(1) You may provide a revised privacy notice, under § 248.8, that covers the customer's new financial product or service; or

(2) If the initial, revised, or annual notice that you most recently provided to that customer was accurate with respect to the new financial product or service, you do not need to provide a new privacy notice under paragraph (a) of this section.

(e) *Exceptions to allow subsequent delivery of notice.* (1) You may provide the initial notice required by paragraph (a)(1) of this section within a reasonable time after you establish a customer relationship if:

(i) Establishing the customer relationship is not at the customer's election;

(ii) Providing notice not later than when you establish a customer relationship would substantially delay the customer's transaction and the customer agrees to receive the notice at a later time; or

(iii) A nonaffiliated broker or dealer or investment adviser establishes a customer relationship between you and a consumer without your prior knowledge.

(2) *Examples of exceptions.* (i) *Not at customer's election.* Establishing a customer relationship is not at the customer's election if the customer's account is transferred to you by a trustee selected by the Securities Investor Protection Corporation ("SIPC") and appointed by a United States Court.

(ii) *Substantial delay of customer's transaction.* Providing notice not later than when you establish a customer relationship would substantially delay the customer's transaction when you and the individual agree over the telephone to enter into a customer relationship involving prompt delivery of the financial product or service.

(iii) *No substantial delay of customer's transaction.* Providing notice not later than when you establish a customer relationship would not substantially delay the customer's transaction when the relationship is initiated in person at your office or through other means by which the customer may view the notice, such as on a web site.

(f) *Delivery.* When you are required to deliver an initial privacy notice by this section, you must deliver it according to § 248.9. If you use a short-form initial notice for non-customers according to § 248.6(d), you may deliver your privacy notice according to § 248.6(d)(3).

[¶ 205] Annual Privacy Notice to Members Required

§ 248.5. (a)(1) *General rule.* You must provide a clear and conspicuous notice to customers that accurately reflects your privacy policies and practices not less than annually during the continuation of the customer relationship. Annually means at least once in any period of 12 consecutive months during which that relationship exists. You may define the 12-consecutive-month period, but you must apply it to the customer on a consistent basis.

(2) *Example.* You provide a notice annually if you define the 12-consecutive-month period as a calendar year and provide the annual notice to the customer once in each calendar year following the calendar year in which you provided the initial notice. For example, if a customer opens an account on any day of year 1, you must provide an annual notice to that customer by December 31 of year 2.

(b)(1) *Termination of customer relationship.* You are not required to provide an annual notice to a former customer.

(2) *Examples.* Your customer becomes a former customer when:

(i) The individual's brokerage account is closed;

(ii) The individual's investment advisory contract is terminated;

(iii) You are an investment company and the individual is no longer the record owner of securities you have issued; or

(iv) You are an investment company and your customer has been determined to be a lost securityholder as defined in 17 CFR 240.17a-24(b).

(c) *Special rule for loans.* If you do not have a customer relationship with a consumer under the special provision for loans in § 248.4(c)(2), then you need not provide an annual notice to that consumer under this section.

(d) *Delivery.* When you are required to deliver an annual privacy notice by this section, you must deliver it according to § 248.9.

[¶ 206] Information to Be Included in Initial and Annual Privacy Notices

§ 248.6. (a) *General rule.* The initial, annual, and revised privacy notices that you provide under §§ 248.4, 248.5, and 248.8 must include each of the following items of information that applies to you or to the consumers to whom you send your privacy notice, in addition to any other information you wish to provide:

(1) The categories of nonpublic personal information that you collect;

(2) The categories of nonpublic personal information that you disclose;

(3) The categories of affiliates and nonaffiliated third parties to whom you disclose nonpublic personal information, other than those parties to whom you disclose information under § § 248.14 and 248.15;

(4) The categories of nonpublic personal information about your former customers that you disclose and the categories of affiliates and nonaffiliated third parties to whom you disclose nonpublic personal information about your former customers, other than those parties to whom you disclose information under § § 248.14 and 248.15;

(5) If you disclose nonpublic personal information to a nonaffiliated third party under § 248.13 (and no other exception applies to that disclosure), a separate statement of the categories of information you disclose and the categories of third parties with whom you have contracted;

(6) An explanation of the consumer's right under § 248.10(a) to opt out of the disclosure of nonpublic personal information to nonaffiliated third parties, including the method(s) by which the consumer may exercise that right at that time;

(7) Any disclosures that you make under section 603(d)(2)(A)(iii) of the Fair Credit Reporting Act (15 U.S.C. 1681a(d)(2)(A)(iii)) (that is, notices regarding the ability to opt out of disclosures of information among affiliates);

(8) Your policies and practices with respect to protecting the confidentiality and security of nonpublic personal information; and

(9) Any disclosure that you make under paragraph (b) of this section.

(b) *Description of nonaffiliated third parties subject to exceptions.* If you disclose nonpublic personal information to third parties as authorized under § § 248.14 and 248.15, you are not required to list those exceptions in the initial or annual privacy notices required by § § 248.4 and 248.5. When describing the categories with respect to those parties, you are required to state only that you make disclosures to other nonaffiliated third parties as permitted by law.

(c) *Examples.* (1) *Categories of nonpublic personal information that you collect.* You satisfy the requirement to categorize the nonpublic personal information that you collect if you list the following categories, as applicable:

(i) Information from the consumer;

(ii) Information about the consumer's transactions with you or your affiliates;

(iii) Information about the consumer's transactions with nonaffiliated third parties; and

(iv) Information from a consumer-reporting agency.

(2) *Categories of nonpublic personal information you disclose.* (i) You satisfy the requirement to categorize the nonpublic personal information that you disclose if you list the categories described in paragraph (e)(1) of this section, as applicable, and a few examples to illustrate the types of information in each category.

(ii) If you reserve the right to disclose all of the nonpublic personal information about consumers that you collect, you may simply state that fact without describing the categories or examples of the nonpublic personal information you disclose.

(3) *Categories of affiliates and nonaffiliated third parties to whom you disclose.* You satisfy the requirement to categorize the affiliates and nonaffiliated third parties to whom you disclose nonpublic personal information if you list the following categories, as applicable, and a few examples to illustrate the types of third parties in each category:

(i) Financial service providers;

(ii) Non-financial companies; and

(iii) Others.

(4) *Disclosures under exception for service providers and joint marketers.* If you disclose nonpublic personal information under the exception in § 248.13 to a nonaffiliated third party to market products or services that you offer alone or jointly with another financial institution, you satisfy the disclosure requirement of paragraph (a)(5) of this section if you:

(i) List the categories of nonpublic personal information you disclose, using the same categories and examples you used to meet the requirements of paragraph (a)(2) of this section, as applicable; and

(ii) State whether the third party is:

(A) A service provider that performs marketing services on your behalf or on behalf of you and another financial institution; or

(B) A financial institution with which you have a joint marketing agreement.

(5) *Simplified notices.* If you do not disclose, and do not wish to reserve the right to disclose, nonpublic personal information to affiliates or nonaffiliated third parties except as authorized under § § 248.14 and 248.15, you may simply state that fact, in addition to the information you must provide under paragraphs (a)(1), (a)(8), (a)(9), and (b) of this section.

(6) *Confidentiality and security.* You describe your policies and practices with respect to protecting the confidentiality and security of nonpublic personal information if you do both of the following:

(i) Describe in general terms who is authorized to have access to the information; and

(ii) State whether you have security practices and procedures in place to ensure the confidentiality of the information in accordance with your policy. You are not required to describe technical information about the safeguards you use.

(d) *Short-form initial notice with opt out notice for non-customers.* (1) You may satisfy the initial notice requirements in § § 248.4(a)(2), 248.7(b), and 248.7(c) for a consumer who is not a customer by providing a short-form initial notice at the same time as you deliver an opt out notice as required in § 248.7.

(2) A short-form initial notice must:

(i) Be clear and conspicuous;

(ii) State that your privacy notice is available upon request; and

(iii) Explain a reasonable means by which the consumer may obtain the privacy notice.

(3) You must deliver your short-form initial notice according to § 248.9. You are not required to deliver your privacy notice with your short-form initial notice. You instead may simply provide the consumer a reasonable means to obtain your privacy notice. If a consumer who receives your short-form notice requests your privacy notice, you must deliver your privacy notice according to § 248.9.

(4) *Examples of obtaining privacy notice.* You provide a reasonable means by which a consumer may obtain a copy of your privacy notice if you:

(i) Provide a toll-free telephone number that the consumer may call to request the notice; or

(ii) For a consumer who conducts business in person at your office, maintain copies of the notice on hand that you provide to the consumer immediately upon request.

(e) *Future disclosures.* Your notice may include:

(1) Categories of nonpublic personal information that you reserve the right to disclose in the future, but do not currently disclose; and

(2) Categories of affiliates or nonaffiliated third parties to whom you reserve the right in the future to disclose, but to whom you do not currently disclose, nonpublic personal information.

(f) *Sample clauses.* Sample clauses illustrating some of the notice content required by this section are included in the Appendix of this part.

[¶ 207] Form of Opt Out Notice to Consumers and Opt Out Methods

§ 248.7. (a)(1) *Form of opt out notice.* If you are required to provide an opt out notice under § 248.10(a), you must provide a clear and conspicuous notice to each of your consumers that accurately explains the right to opt out under that section. The notice must state:

(i) That you disclose or reserve the right to disclose nonpublic personal information about your consumer to a nonaffiliated third party;

(ii) That the consumer has the right to opt out of that disclosure; and

(iii) A reasonable means by which the consumer may exercise the opt out right.

(2) *Examples.* (i) *Adequate opt out notice.* You provide adequate notice that the consumer can opt out of the disclosure of nonpublic personal information to a nonaffiliated third party if you:

(A) Identify all of the categories of nonpublic personal information that you disclose or reserve the right to disclose, and all of the categories of nonaffiliated third parties to which you disclose the information, as described in § 248.6(a)(2) and (3) and state that the consumer can opt out of the disclosure of that information; and

(B) Identify the financial products or services that the consumer obtains from you, either singly or jointly, to which the opt out direction would apply.

(ii) *Reasonable opt out means.* You provide a reasonable means to exercise an opt out right if you:

(A) Designate check-off boxes in a prominent position on the relevant forms with the opt out notice;

(B) Include a reply form together with the opt out notice;

(C) Provide an electronic means to opt out, such as a form that can be sent via electronic mail or a process at your web site, if the consumer agrees to the electronic delivery of information; or

(D) Provide a toll-free telephone number that consumers may call to opt out.

(iii) *Unreasonable opt out means.* You *do not* provide a reasonable means of opting out if:

(A) The only means of opting out is for the consumer to write his or her own letter to exercise that opt out right; or

(B) The only means of opting out as described in any notice subsequent to the initial notice is to use a check-off box that you provided with the initial notice but did not include with the subsequent notice.

(iv) *Specific opt out means.* You may require each consumer to opt out through a specific means, as long as that means is reasonable for that consumer.

(b) *Same form as initial notice permitted.* You may provide the opt out notice together with or on the same written or electronic form as the initial notice you provide in accordance with § 248.4.

(c) *Initial notice required when opt out notice delivered subsequent to initial notice.* If you provide the opt out notice after the initial notice in accordance with § 248.4, you must also include a copy of the initial notice with the opt out notice in writing or, if the consumer agrees, electronically.

(d) *Joint relationships.* (1) If two or more consumers jointly obtain a financial product or service from you, you may provide a single opt out notice. Your opt out notice must explain how you will treat an opt out direction by a joint consumer.

(2) Any of the joint consumers may exercise the right to opt out. You may either:

(i) Treat an opt out direction by a joint consumer as applying to all of the associated joint consumers; or

(ii) Permit each joint consumer to opt out separately.

(3) If you permit each joint consumer to opt out separately, you must permit one of the joint consumers to opt out on behalf of all of the joint consumers.

(4) You may not require *all* joint consumers to opt out before you implement any opt out direction.

(5) *Example.* If John and Mary have a joint brokerage account with you and arrange for you to send statements to John's address, you may do any of the following, but you must explain in your opt out notice which opt out policy you will follow:

(i) Send a single opt out notice to John's address, but you must accept an opt out direction from either John or Mary;

(ii) Treat an opt out direction by either John or Mary as applying to the entire account. If you do so, and John opts out, you may not require Mary to opt out as well before implementing John's opt out direction; or

(iii) Permit John and Mary to make different opt out directions. If you do so:

(A) You must permit John and Mary to opt out for each other.

(B) If both opt out, you must permit both to notify you in a single response (such as on a form or through a telephone call).

(C) If John opts out and Mary does not, you may only disclose nonpublic personal information about Mary, but not about John and not about John and Mary jointly.

(e) *Time to comply with opt out.* You must comply with a consumer's opt out direction as soon as reasonably practicable after you receive it.

(f) *Continuing right to opt out.* A consumer may exercise the right to opt out at any time.

(g) *Duration of consumer's opt out direction.* (1) A consumer's direction to opt out under this section is effective until the consumer revokes it in writing or, if the consumer agrees, electronically.

(2) When a customer relationship terminates, the customer's opt out direction continues to apply to the nonpublic personal information that you collected during or related to that relationship. If the individual subsequently establishes a new customer relationship with you, the opt out direction that applied to the former relationship does not apply to the new relationship.

(h) *Delivery.* When you are required to deliver an opt out notice by this section, you must deliver it according to § 248.9.

[¶ 208] Revised Privacy Notices

§ 248.8. (a) *General rule.* Except as otherwise authorized in this part, you must not, directly or through any affiliate, disclose any nonpublic personal information about a consumer to a nonaffiliated third party other than as described in the initial notice that you provided to that consumer under § 248.4, unless:

(1) You have provided to the consumer a clear and conspicuous revised notice that accurately describes your policies and practices;

(2) You have provided to the consumer a new opt out notice;

(3) You have given the consumer a reasonable opportunity, before you disclose the information to the nonaffiliated third party, to opt out of the disclosure; and

(4) The consumer does not opt out.

(b) *Examples.* (1) Except as otherwise permitted by §§ 248.13, 248.14, and 248.15, you must provide a revised notice before you:

(i) Disclose a new category of nonpublic personal information to any nonaffiliated third party;

(ii) Disclose nonpublic personal information to a new category of nonaffiliated third party; or

(iii) Disclose nonpublic personal information about a former customer to a nonaffiliated third party, if that former customer has not had the opportunity to exercise an opt out right regarding that disclosure.

(2) A revised notice is not required if you disclose nonpublic personal information to a new nonaffiliated third party that you adequately described in your prior notice.

(c) *Delivery.* When you are required to deliver a revised privacy notice by this section, you must deliver it according to § 248.9.

[¶ 209] Delivering Privacy and Opt Out Notices

§ 248.9. (a) *How to provide notices.* You must provide any privacy notices and opt out notices, including short-form initial notices that this part requires so that each consumer can reasonably be expected to receive actual notice in writing or, if the consumer agrees, electronically.

(b)(1) *Examples of reasonable expectation of actual notice.* You may reasonably expect that a consumer will receive actual notice if you:

(i) Hand-deliver a printed copy of the notice to the consumer;

(ii) Mail a printed copy of the notice to the last known address of the consumer;

(iii) For the consumer who conducts transactions electronically, post the notice on the electronic site and require the consumer to acknowledge receipt of the notice as a necessary step to obtaining a particular financial product or service; or

(iv) For an isolated transaction with the consumer, such as an ATM transaction, post the notice on the ATM screen and require the consumer to acknowledge receipt of the notice as a necessary step to obtaining the particular financial product or service.

(2) *Examples of unreasonable expectation of actual notice.* You may not, however, reasonably expect that a consumer will receive actual notice of your privacy policies and practices if you:

(i) Only post a sign in your branch or office or generally publish advertisements of your privacy policies and practices; or

(ii) Send the notice via electronic mail to a consumer who does not obtain a financial product or service from you electronically.

(c) *Annual notices only.* (1) You may reasonably expect that a customer will receive actual notice of your annual privacy notice if:

(i) The customer uses your web site to access financial products and services electronically and agrees to receive notices at the web site and you post your current privacy notice continuously in a clear and conspicuous manner on the web site; or

(ii) The customer has requested that you refrain from sending any information regarding the customer relationship, and your current privacy notice remains available to the customer upon request.

(2) *Example of reasonable expectation of receipt of annual privacy notice.* You may reasonably expect that consumers who share an address will receive actual notice of your annual privacy notice if you deliver the notice with or in a stockholder or shareholder report under the conditions in 17 CFR 270.30d-1(f) or 17 CFR 270.30d-2(b), or with or in a prospectus under the conditions in 17 CFR 230.154.

(d) *Oral description of notice insufficient.* You may not provide any notice required by this part solely by orally explaining the notice, either in person or over the telephone.

(e) *Retention or accessibility of notices for customers.* (1) For customers only, you must provide the initial notice required by § 248.4(a)(1), the annual notice required by § 248.5(a), and the revised notice required by § 248.8, so that the customer can retain them or obtain them later in writing or, if the customer agrees, electronically.

(2) *Examples of retention or accessibility.* You provide a privacy notice to the customer so that the customer can retain it or obtain it later if you:

(i) Hand-deliver a printed copy of the notice to the customer;

(ii) Mail a printed copy of the notice to the last known address of the customer; or

(iii) Make your current privacy notice available on a web site (or a link to another web site) for the customer who obtains a financial product or service electronically and agrees to receive the notice at the web site.

(f) *Joint notice with other financial institutions.* You may provide a joint notice from you and one or more of your affiliates or other financial institutions, as identified in the notice, as long as the notice is accurate with respect to you and the other institutions.

(g) *Joint relationships.* If two or more consumers jointly obtain a financial product or service from you, you may satisfy the initial, annual, and revised notice requirements of paragraph (a) of this section by providing one notice to those consumers jointly.

Subpart B—Limits on Disclosures

[¶ 210] Limits on Disclosure of Nonpublic Personal Information to Nonaffiliated Third Parties

§ 248.10. (a)(1) *Conditions for disclosure.* Except as otherwise authorized in this part, you may not, directly or through any affiliate, disclose any nonpublic personal information about a consumer to a nonaffiliated third party unless:

(i) You have provided to the consumer an initial notice as required under § 248.4;

(ii) You have provided to the consumer an opt out notice as required in § 248.7;

(iii) You have given the consumer a reasonable opportunity, before you disclose the information to the nonaffiliated third party, to opt out of the disclosure; and

(iv) The consumer does not opt out.

(2) *Opt out definition.* Opt out means a direction by the consumer that you not disclose nonpublic personal information about that consumer to a nonaffiliated third party, other than as permitted by § § 248.13, 248.14, and 248.15.

(3) *Examples of reasonable opportunity to opt out.* You provide a consumer with a reasonable opportunity to opt out if:

(i) *By mail.* You mail the notices required in paragraph (a)(1) of this section to the consumer and allow the consumer to opt out by mailing a form, calling a toll-free telephone number, or any other reasonable means within 30 days after the date you mailed the notices.

(ii) *By electronic means.* A customer opens an on-line account with you and agrees to receive the notices required in paragraph (a)(1) of this section electronically, and you allow the customer to opt out by any reasonable means within 30 days after the date that the customer acknowledges receipt of the notices in conjunction with opening the account.

(iii) *Isolated transaction with consumer.* For an isolated transaction, such as the provision of brokerage services to a consumer as an accommodation, you provide the consumer with a reasonable opportunity to opt out if you provide the notices required in paragraph (a)(1) of this section at the time of the transaction and request that the consumer decide, as a necessary part of the transaction, whether to opt out before completing the transaction.

(b) *Application of opt out to all consumers and all nonpublic personal information.* (1) You must comply with this section, regardless of whether you and the consumer have established a customer relationship.

(2) Unless you comply with this section, you may not, directly or through any affiliate, disclose any nonpublic personal information about a consumer that you have collected, regardless of whether you collected it before or after receiving the direction to opt out from the consumer.

(c) *Partial opt out.* You may allow a consumer to select certain nonpublic personal information or certain nonaffiliated third parties with respect to which the consumer wishes to opt out.

[¶ 211] Limits on Redisclosure and Reuse of Information

§ 248.11. (a)(1) *Information you receive under an exception.* If you receive nonpublic personal information from a nonaffiliated financial institution under an exception in § 248.14 or 248.15, your disclosure and use of that information is limited as follows:

(i) You may disclose the information to the affiliates of the financial institution from which you received the information;

(ii) You may disclose the information to your affiliates, but your affiliates may, in turn, disclose and use the information only to the extent that you may disclose and use the information; and

(iii) You may disclose and use the information pursuant to an exception in § 248.14 or 248.15 in the ordinary course of business to carry out the activity covered by the exception under which you received the information.

(2) *Example.* If you receive a customer list from a nonaffiliated financial institution in order to provide account-processing services under the exception in § 248.14(a), you may disclose that information under any exception in § 248.14 or 248.15 in the ordinary course of business in order to provide those services. You could also disclose that information in response to a properly authorized subpoena or in the ordinary course of business to your attorneys, accountants, and auditors. You could not disclose that information to a third party for marketing purposes or use that information for your own marketing purposes.

(b)(1) *Information you receive outside of an exception.* If you receive nonpublic personal information from a nonaffiliated financial institution other than under an exception in § 248.14 or 248.15, you may disclose the information only:

(i) To the affiliates of the financial institution from which you received the information;

(ii) To your affiliates, but your affiliates may, in turn, disclose the information only to the extent that you can disclose the information; and

(iii) To any other person, if the disclosure would be lawful if made directly to that person by the financial institution from which you received the information.

(2) *Example.* If you obtain a customer list from a nonaffiliated financial institution outside of the exceptions in § § 248.14 and 248.15:

(i) You may use that list for your own purposes;

(ii) You may disclose that list to another nonaffiliated third party only if the financial institution from which you purchased the list could have lawfully disclosed the list to that third party. That is, you may disclose the list in accordance with the privacy policy of the financial institution from which you received the list, as limited by the opt out direction of each consumer whose nonpublic personal information you intend to disclose, and you may disclose the list in accordance with an exception in § 248.14 or 248.15, such as in the ordinary course of business to your attorneys, accountants, or auditors.

(c) *Information you disclose under an exception.* If you disclose nonpublic personal information to a nonaffiliated third party under an exception in § 248.14 or 248.15, the third party may disclose and use that information only as follows:

(1) The third party may disclose the information to your affiliates;

(2) The third party may disclose the information to its affiliates, but its affiliates may, in turn, disclose and use the information only to the extent that the third party may disclose and use the information; and

(3) The third party may disclose and use the information pursuant to an exception in § 248.14 or 248.15 in the ordinary course of business to carry out the activity covered by the exception under which it received the information.

(d) *Information you disclose outside of an exception.* If you disclose nonpublic personal information to a nonaffiliated third party other than under an exception in § 248.14 or 248.15, the third party may disclose the information only:

(1) To your affiliates;

(2) To its affiliates, but its affiliates, in turn, may disclose the information only to the extent the third party can disclose the information; and

(3) To any other person, if the disclosure would be lawful if you made it directly to that person.

[¶ 212] Limits on Sharing of Account Number Information for Marketing Purposes

§ 248.12. (a) *General prohibition on disclosure of account numbers.* You must not, directly or through an affiliate, disclose, other than to a consumer reporting agency, an account number or similar form of access number or access code for a consumer's credit card account, deposit account, or transaction account to any nonaffiliated third party for use in telemarketing, direct mail marketing, or other marketing through electronic mail to the consumer.

(b) *Exceptions.* Paragraph (a) of this section does not apply if you disclose an account number or similar form of access number or access code:

(1) To your agent or service provider solely in order to perform marketing for your own products or services, as long as the agent or service provider is not authorized to directly initiate charges to the account; or

(2) To a participant in a private label credit card program or an affinity or similar program where the participants in the program are identified to the customer when the customer enters into the program.

(c) *Example-Account number.* An account number, or similar form of access number or access code, does not include a number or code in an encrypted form, as long as you do not provide the recipient with a means to decode the number or code.

Subpart C—Exceptions

[¶ 213] Exception to Opt Out Requirements for Service Providers and Joint Marketing

§ 248.13. (a) *General rule.* (1) The opt out requirements in § § 248.7 and 248.10 do not apply when you provide nonpublic personal information to a nonaffiliated third party to perform services for you or functions on your behalf, if you:

(i) Provide the initial notice in accordance with § 248.4; and

(ii) Enter into a contractual agreement with the third party that prohibits the third party from disclosing or using the information other than to carry out the purposes for which you disclosed the information, including use under an exception in § 248.14 or 248.15 in the ordinary course of business to carry out those purposes.

(2) *Example.* If you disclose nonpublic personal information under this section to a financial institution with which you perform joint marketing, your contractual agreement with that institution meets the requirements of paragraph (a)(1)(ii) of this section if it prohibits the institution from disclosing or using the nonpublic personal information except as necessary to carry out the joint marketing or under an exception in § 248.14 or 248.15 in the ordinary course of business to carry out that joint marketing.

(b) *Service may include joint marketing.* The services a nonaffiliated third party performs for you under paragraph (a) of this section may include marketing of your own products or services or marketing of financial products or services offered pursuant to joint agreements between you and one or more financial institutions.

(c) *Definition of joint agreement.* For purposes of this section, joint agreement means a written contract pursuant to which you and one or more financial institutions jointly offer, endorse, or sponsor a financial product or service.

[¶ 214] Exceptions to Notice and Opt Out Requirements for Processing and Servicing Transactions

§ 248.14. (a) *Exceptions for processing and servicing transactions at consumer's request.* The requirements for initial notice in § 248.4(a)(2), for the opt out in § § 248.7 and 248.10, and for initial notice in § 248.13 in connection with service providers and joint marketing, do not apply if you disclose nonpublic personal information as necessary to effect, administer, or enforce a transaction that a consumer requests or authorizes, or in connection with:

(1) Processing or servicing a financial product or service that a consumer requests or authorizes;

(2) Maintaining or servicing the consumer's account with you, or with another entity as part of a private label credit card program or other extension of credit on behalf of such entity; or

(3) A proposed or actual securitization, secondary market sale (including sales of servicing rights), or similar transaction related to a transaction of the consumer.

(b) *Necessary to effect, administer, or enforce a transaction* means that the disclosure is:

(1) Required, or is one of the lawful or appropriate methods, to enforce your rights or the rights of other persons engaged in carrying out the financial transaction or providing the product or service; or

(2) Required, or is a usual, appropriate, or acceptable method:

(i) To carry out the transaction or the product or service business of which the transaction is a part, and record, service, or maintain the consumer's account in the ordinary course of providing the financial service or financial product;

(ii) To administer or service benefits or claims relating to the transaction or the product or service business of which it is a part;

(iii) To provide a confirmation, statement, or other record of the transaction, or information on the status or value of the financial service or financial product to the consumer or the consumer's agent or broker;

(iv) To accrue or recognize incentives or bonuses associated with the transaction that are provided by you or any other party;

(v) To underwrite insurance at the consumer's request or for reinsurance purposes, or for any of the following purposes as they relate to a consumer's insurance: account administration, reporting, investigating, or preventing fraud or material misrepresentation, processing premium payments, processing insurance claims, administering insurance benefits (including utilization review activities), participating in research projects, or as otherwise required or specifically permitted by federal or State law; or

(vi) In connection with:

(A) The authorization, settlement, billing, processing, clearing, transferring, reconciling or collection of amounts charged, debited, or otherwise paid using a debit, credit, or other payment card, check, or account number, or by other payment means;

(B) The transfer of receivables, accounts, or interests therein; or

(C) The audit of debit, credit, or other payment information.

[¶ 215] Other Exceptions to Notice and Opt Out Requirements

§ 248.15. (a) *Exceptions to notice and opt out requirements.* The requirements for initial notice in § 248.4(a)(2), for the opt out in § § 248.7 and 248.10, and for initial notice in § 248.13 in connection with service providers and joint marketing do not apply when you disclose nonpublic personal information:

(1) With the consent or at the direction of the consumer, provided that the consumer has not revoked the consent or direction;

(2)(i) To protect the confidentiality or security of your records pertaining to the consumer, service, product, or transaction;

(ii) To protect against or prevent actual or potential fraud, unauthorized transactions, claims, or other liability;

(iii) For required institutional risk control or for resolving consumer disputes or inquiries;

(iv) To persons holding a legal or beneficial interest relating to the consumer; or

(v) To persons acting in a fiduciary or representative capacity on behalf of the consumer;

(3) To provide information to insurance rate advisory organizations, guaranty funds or agencies, agencies that are rating you, persons that are assessing your compliance with industry standards, and your attorneys, accountants, and auditors;

(4) To the extent specifically permitted or required under other provisions of law and in accordance with the Right to Financial Privacy Act of 1978 (12 U.S.C. 3401 *et seq.*), to law enforcement agencies (including a federal functional regulator, the Secretary of the Treasury, with respect to 31 U.S.C. Chapter 53, Subchapter II (Records and Reports on Monetary Instruments and Transactions) and 12 U.S.C. Chapter 21 (Financial Recordkeeping), a State insurance authority, with respect to any person domiciled in that insurance authority's State that is engaged in providing insurance, and the Federal Trade Commission), self-regulatory organizations, or for an investigation on a matter related to public safety;

(5)(i) To a consumer reporting agency in accordance with the Fair Credit Reporting Act (15 U.S.C. 1681 *et seq.*), or

(ii) From a consumer report reported by a consumer reporting agency;

(6) In connection with a proposed or actual sale, merger, transfer, or exchange of all or a portion of a business or operating unit if the disclosure of nonpublic personal information concerns solely consumers of such business or unit; or

(7)(i) To comply with federal, State, or local laws, rules and other applicable legal requirements;

(ii) To comply with a properly authorized civil, criminal, or regulatory investigation, or subpoena or summons by federal, State, or local authorities; or

(iii) To respond to judicial process or government regulatory authorities having jurisdiction over you for examination, compliance, or other purposes as authorized by law.

(b) *Examples of consent and revocation of consent.* (1) A consumer may specifically consent to your disclosure to a nonaffiliated mortgage lender of the value of the assets in the consumer's brokerage or investment advisory account so that the lender can evaluate the consumer's application for a mortgage loan.

(2) A consumer may revoke consent by subsequently exercising the right to opt out of future disclosures of nonpublic personal information as permitted under § 248.7(f).

Subpart D—Relation to other Laws; Effective Date

[¶ 216] Protection of Fair Credit Reporting Act

§ 248.16. Nothing in this part shall be construed to modify, limit, or supersede the operation of the Fair Credit Reporting Act (15 U.S.C. 1681 *et seq.*), and no inference shall be drawn on the basis of the provisions of this part regarding whether information is transaction or experience information under section 603 of that Act.

[¶ 217] Relation to State Laws

§ 248.17. (a) *In general.* This part shall not be construed as superseding, altering, or affecting any statute, regulation, order, or interpretation in effect in any State, except to the extent that such State statute, regulation, order, or interpretation is inconsistent with the provisions of this part, and then only to the extent of the inconsistency.

(b) *Greater protection under State law.* For purposes of this section, a State statute, regulation, order, or interpretation is not inconsistent with the provisions of this part if the protection such statute, regulation, order, or interpretation affords any consumer is greater than the protection provided under this part, as determined by the Federal Trade Commission, after consultation with the Commission, on the Federal Trade Commission's own motion, or upon the petition of any interested party.

[¶ 218] Effective Date; Transition Rule

§ 248.18. (a) *Effective date.* This part is effective November 13, 2000. In order to provide sufficient time for you to establish policies and systems to comply with the requirements of this part, the compliance date for this part is July 1, 2001.

(b)(1) *Notice requirement for consumers who are your customers on the compliance date.* By July 1, 2001, you must have provided an initial notice, as required by § 248.4, to consumers who are your customers on July 1, 2001.

(2) *Example.* You provide an initial notice to consumers who are your customers on July 1, 2001, if, by that date, you have established a system for providing an initial notice to all new customers and have mailed the initial notice to all your existing customers.

(c) *Two-year grandfathering of service agreements.* Until July 1, 2002, a contract that you have entered into with a nonaffiliated third party to perform services for you or functions on your behalf satisfies the provisions of § 248.13(a)(2), even if the contract does not include a requirement that the third party maintain the confidentiality of nonpublic personal information, as long as you entered into the agreement on or before July 1, 2000.

§ § 248.19—248.29 [Reserved]

[¶ 219] Procedures to Safeguard Customer Records and Information

§ 248.30. Procedures to safeguard customer records and information. Every broker, dealer, and investment company, and every investment adviser registered with the Commission must adopt policies and procedures that address administrative, technical, and physical safeguards for the protection of customer records and information. These policies and procedures must be reasonably designed to:

(a) Insure the security and confidentiality of customer records and information;

(b) Protect against any anticipated threats or hazards to the security or integrity of customer records and information; and

(c) Protect against unauthorized access to or use of customer records or information that could result in substantial harm or inconvenience to any customer.

Appendix to Part 248

[¶ 220] Sample Clauses

§ 248.1 et seq. Appendix. Financial institutions, including a group of financial holding company affiliates that use a common privacy notice, may use the following sample clauses, if the clause is accurate for each institution that uses the notice. (Note that disclosure of certain information, such as assets, income, and information from a consumer reporting agency, may give rise to obligations under the Fair Credit Reporting Act, such as a requirement to permit a consumer to opt out of disclosures to affiliates or designation as a consumer reporting agency if disclosures are made to nonaffiliated third parties.)

A-1-Categories of information you collect (all institutions)

You may use this clause, as applicable, to meet the requirement of § 248.6(a)(1) to describe the categories of nonpublic personal information you collect.

Sample Clause A-1:

We collect nonpublic personal information about you from the following sources:

- Information we receive from you on applications or other forms;
- Information about your transactions with us, our affiliates, or others; and
- Information we receive from a consumer reporting agency.

A-2-Categories of information you disclose (institutions that disclose outside of the exceptions)

You may use one of these clauses, as applicable, to meet the requirement of § 248.6(a)(2) to describe the categories of nonpublic personal information you disclose. You may use these clauses if you disclose nonpublic personal information other than as permitted by the exceptions in § § 248.13, 248.14, and 248.15.

Sample Clause A-2, Alternative 1:

We may disclose the following kinds of nonpublic personal information about you:

- Information we receive from you on applications or other forms, such as [*provide illustrative examples, such as "your name, address, social security number, assets, and income"*];
- Information about your transactions with us, our affiliates, or others, such as [*provide illustrative examples, such as "your account balance, payment history, parties to transactions, and credit card usage"*]; and
- Information we receive from a consumer reporting agency, such as [*provide illustrative examples, such as "your creditworthiness and credit history"*].

Sample Clause A-2, Alternative 2:

We may disclose all of the information that we collect, as described [*describe location in the notice, such as "above" or "below"*].

A-3-Categories of information you disclose and parties to whom you disclose (institutions that do not disclose outside of the exceptions)

You may use this clause, as applicable, to meet the requirements of § § 248.6(a)(2), (3), and (4) to describe the categories of nonpublic personal information about customers and former customers that you disclose and the categories of affiliates and nonaffiliated third parties to whom you disclose. You may use this clause if you do not disclose nonpublic personal information to any party, other than as permitted by the exceptions in § § 248.14 and 248.15.

Sample Clause A-3:

We do not disclose any nonpublic personal information about our customers or former customers to anyone, except as permitted by law.

A-4-Categories of parties to whom you disclose (institutions that disclose outside of the exceptions)

You may use this clause, as applicable, to meet the requirement of § 248.6(a)(3) to describe the categories of affiliates and nonaffiliated third parties to whom you disclose nonpublic personal information. You may use this clause if you disclose nonpublic personal information other than as permitted by the exceptions in § § 248.13, 248.14, and 248.15, as well as when permitted by the exceptions in § § 248.14 and 248.15.

Sample Clause A-4:

We may disclose nonpublic personal information about you to the following types of third parties:

- Financial service providers, such as [*provide illustrative examples, such as "mortgage bankers, securities broker-dealers, and insurance agents"*];

- Non-financial companies, such as [*provide illustrative examples, such as "retailers, direct marketers, airlines, and publishers"*]; and

- Others, such as [*provide illustrative examples, such as "non-profit organizations"*].

We may also disclose nonpublic personal information about you to nonaffiliated third parties as permitted by law.

A-5-Service provider/joint marketing exception

You may use one of these clauses, as applicable, to meet the requirements of § 248.6(a)(5) related to the exception for service providers and joint marketers in § 248.13. If you disclose nonpublic personal information under this exception, you must describe the categories of nonpublic personal information you disclose and the categories of third parties with whom you have contracted.

Sample Clause A-5, Alternative 1:

We may disclose the following information to companies that perform marketing services on our behalf or to other financial institutions with which we have joint marketing agreements:

- Information we receive from you on applications or other forms, such as [*provide illustrative examples, such as "your name, address, social security number, assets, and income"*];

- Information about your transactions with us, our affiliates, or others, such as [*provide illustrative examples, such as "your account balance, payment history, parties to transactions, and credit card usage"*]; and

- Information we receive from a consumer reporting agency, such as [*provide illustrative examples, such as "your creditworthiness and credit history"*].

Sample Clause A-5, Alternative 2:

We may disclose all of the information we collect, as described [*describe location in the notice, such as "above" or "below"*] to companies that perform marketing services on our behalf or to other financial institutions with whom we have joint marketing agreements.

A-6-Explanation of opt out right (institutions that disclose outside of the exceptions)

You may use this clause, as applicable, to meet the requirement of § 248.6(a)(6) to provide an explanation of the consumer's right to opt out of the disclosure of nonpublic personal information to nonaffiliated third parties, including the method(s) by which the consumer may exercise that right. You may use this clause if you disclose nonpublic personal information other than as permitted by the exceptions in § § 248.13, 248.14, and 248.15.

Sample Clause A-6:

If you prefer that we not disclose nonpublic personal information about you to nonaffiliated third parties, you may opt out of those disclosures, that is, you may direct us not to make those disclosures (other than disclosures permitted by law). If you wish to opt out of disclosures to nonaffiliated third parties, you may [*describe a reasonable means of opting out, such as "call the following toll-free number: (insert number)"*].

A-7-Confidentiality and security (all institutions)

You may use this clause, as applicable, to meet the requirement of § 248.6(a)(8) to describe your policies and practices with respect to protecting the confidentiality and security of nonpublic personal information.

Sample Clause A-7:

We restrict access to nonpublic personal information about you to [*provide an appropriate description, such as "those employees who need to know that information to provide products or services to you"*]. We maintain physical, electronic, and procedural safeguards that comply with federal standards to guard your nonpublic personal information.

Topical Index

References are to paragraph numbers

A

Account numbers
. encryption . . . 115
. information sharing . . . 115
. marketing exception . . . 115
. private label credit cards . . . 115

Affiliates
. defined . . . 103

Annual privacy notice
. contents
. . affiliates and third parties . . . 106
. . confidentiality safeguards . . . 106
. . Fair Credit Reporting Act . . . 106
. . former customers . . . 106
. . future disclosures . . . 106
. . joint marketing arrangements . . . 106
. . personal information collected . . . 106
. . personal information disclosed . . . 106
. . right to opt out . . . 106
. . sample clauses . . . 220
. delivery
. . householding . . . 109
. . joint notice . . . 109
. . joint relationships . . . 109
. . multiple accounts . . . 109
. . recordkeeping . . . 109
. . retention . . . 109
. requirements . . . 105
. sample clauses . . . 220

B

Broker-dealers
. defined . . . 101; 103
. foreign institutions . . . 101
. foreign offices . . . 101

C

Clear and conspicuous
. defined . . . 103

Collect
. defined . . . 103

Company
. defined . . . 103

Consumer
. customer distinguished . . . 103
. defined . . . 103

Consumer reporting agency
. defined . . . 103

Control
. defined . . . 103

Credit cards
. information sharing
. . account numbers . . . 115
. . private label cards . . . 115

Customer
. consumer distinguished . . . 103

Customer—continued
. defined . . . 103
. one-time transactions . . . 103

Customer relationship
. commencement . . . 104
. defined . . . 104

D

Definitions
. affiliates . . . 103
. broker-dealers . . . 101; 103
. clear and conspicuous . . . 103
. collect . . . 103
. company . . . 103
. consumer . . . 103
. consumer reporting agency . . . 103
. control . . . 103
. customer . . . 103
. customer relationship . . . 104
. federal functional regulator . . . 103
. financial institution . . . 103
. financial product or service . . . 103
. investment advisers . . . 103
. investment companies . . . 103
. nonpublic personal information . . 103
. personally identifiable financial information . . . 103
. publicly available information . . . 103

E

Encryption
. account numbers
. . information sharing . . . 115

Exceptions
. joint marketing . . . 111
. opt out
. . administering claims and benefits . . . 112
. . confirmation statements . . . 112
. . consent exception . . . 113
. . insurance underwriting . . . 112
. . joint marketing arrangements . . . 111
. . processing and serving transactions . . . 112
. . resolving customer disputes . . . 113
. . resolving customer inquiries . . . 113
. . securitization . . . 112
. . settling a transaction . . . 112

F

Fair Credit Reporting Act
. initial and annual privacy notices . . . 106
. modification by privacy rules . . . 116

Federal functional regulator
. defined . . . 103

Financial institution
. defined . . . 103

Financial product or service
. defined . . . 103

Foreign institutions
. privacy rules . . . 101

Foreign offices
. SEC-registered institutions . . . 101

G

Gramm-Leach-Bliley Act
. privacy provisions in general . . . 101
. SEC mandate . . . 101

I

Initial privacy notice
. closed-end funds . . . 104
. concomitant notices . . . 104
. contents
. . affiliates and third parties . . . 106
. . confidentiality safeguards . . . 106
. . Fair Credit Reporting Act . . . 106
. . former customers . . . 106
. . future disclosures . . . 106
. . joint marketing arrangements . . . 106
. . personal information collected . . . 106
. . personal information disclosed . . . 106
. . right to opt out . . . 106
. . sample clauses . . . 220
. delivery
. . delayed delivery . . . 104
. . householding . . . 109
. . joint notice . . . 109
. . joint relationships . . . 109
. . multiple accounts . . . 109
. . recordkeeping . . . 109
. . retention . . . 109
. joint account holders . . . 104
. mergers . . . 104
. mutual funds . . . 104
. one-time transactions . . . 104
. requirements . . . 104
. sample clauses . . . 220
. short-form notice . . . 104

Insurance
. privacy rules
. . variable annuities . . . 101
. . variable life insurance . . . 101

Internet
. clear and conspicuous disclosure . . . 103
. consumers
. . use of financial tools . . . 103

Investment advisers
. defined . . . 103
. foreign institutions . . . 101
. foreign offices . . . 101
. pension plans . . . 103
. wrap accounts . . . 103

Investment companies
. closed-end funds . . . 104
. defined . . . 101; 103
. initial privacy notice . . . 104
. foreign institutions . . . 101
. foreign offices . . . 101

L

Loans
. consumers . . . 103
. customers . . . 103

M

Marketing
. joint marketing arrangements
. . information in notices . . . 106
. . opt-out exception . . . 111

Mergers
. initial privacy notice . . . 104

N

Nonpublic personal information
. defined . . . 103

Notice
. opt-out notice . . . 107
. privacy notice
. . annual . . . 105
. . initial . . . 104
. . revised . . . 108
. . short-form . . . 104
. sample clauses . . . 220

O

Opt out
. exceptions
. . administering claims and benefits . . . 112
. . confirmation statements . . . 112
. . consent exception . . . 113
. . insurance underwriting . . . 112
. . joint marketing arrangements . . . 111
. . processing and serving transactions . . . 112
. . resolving customer disputes . . . 113
. . resolving customer inquiries . . . 113
. . securitization . . . 112
. . settling a transaction . . . 112
. investment advisers
. . execution by brokers . . . 112
. joint marketing arrangements
. . exception . . . 111
. right to opt out
. . initial notice . . . 107
. . isolated transactions . . . 110
. . joint accounts . . . 107
. . partial opt out . . . 110
. . reasonable means . . . 107; 110
. . revised notices . . . 108
. . sample clause . . . 220
. . specific means and duration . . . 107

P

Pension plans
. investment advisers
. . customers . . . 103

Personally identifiable financial information
. defined . . . 103

Preemption
. state laws . . . 117

Privacy protection standards
. confidentiality issues . . . 118
. policies and procedures . . . 118
. security issues . . . 118

Publicly available information
. defined . . . 103

R

Regulation S-P
. appendix . . . 220
. compliance
. . guidance for certain entities . . . 119
. interaction with other laws
. . Fair Credit Reporting Act . . . 116
. . state laws . . . 117
. purposes . . . 101
. sample clauses . . . 220
. scope . . . 101
. statutory basis . . . 101
. text of rules . . . 201–219

S

Safe harbors
. privacy rules . . . 102

Sample clauses
. discussion . . . 102
. text . . . 220

Securities and Exchange Commission
. guidance for certain entities . . . 119
. statutory mandate . . . 101

State laws
. preemption . . . 117

T

Third-party monitoring
. financial institutions
. . execution of transactions . . . 114

Trusts
. consumers . . . 103
. customers . . . 103

V

Variable annuities
. privacy rules . . . 101

Variable life insurance
. privacy rules . . . 101

W

Wrap accounts
. investment advisers
. . customers . . . 103